W9-ATI-370

WORLD
HISTORY SERIES ■■■

The
Reformation

Titles in the World History Series

The Reformation

by
Sarah Flowers

Lucent Books, P.O. Box 289011, San Diego, CA 92198-9011

Library of Congress Cataloging-in-Publication Data

Flowers, Sarah, 1952–
    The Reformation / by Sarah Flowers
       p. cm.—(World history series)
    Includes bibliographical references and index.
    Summary: Historical overview of the Protestant
Reformation from its initial stirrings in medieval times
through the Counter-Reformation, and its cultural effects.
    ISBN 1-56006-243-6 (lib. bdg. : alk. paper)
    1. Reformation—Juvenile literature. 2. Counter-
Reformation—Juvenile literature. [1.Christianity—History.]
I.Title. II. Series.
BR308.F47   1996
270.6—dc20   95-8822
                                             CIP
                                             AC

Copyright 1996 by Lucent Books, Inc., P.O. Box 289011,
San Diego, California 92198-9011

Printed in the U.S.A.

No part of this book may be reproduced or used in any other
form or by any other means, electrical, mechanical, or otherwise, including, but not limited to, photocopy, recording, or
any information storage and retrieval system without prior
written permission from the publisher.

270.6 FLO 1996

Flowers, Sarah.
The Reformation.

Contents

cooks books $16.97

7-16/01

Foreword

Each year on the first day of school, nearly every history teacher faces the task of explaining why his or her students should study history. One logical answer to this question is that exploring what happened in our past explains how the things we often take for granted—our customs, ideas, and institutions—came to be. As statesman and historian Winston Churchill put it, "Every nation or group of nations has its own tale to tell. Knowledge of the trials and struggles is necessary to all who would comprehend the problems, perils, challenges, and opportunities which confront us today." Thus, a study of history puts modern ideas and institutions in perspective. For example, though the founders of the United States were talented and creative thinkers, they clearly did not invent the concept of democracy. Instead, they adapted some democratic ideas that had originated in ancient Greece and with which the Romans, the British, and others had experimented. An exploration of these cultures, then, reveals their very real connection to us through institutions that continue to shape our daily lives.

Another reason often given for studying history is the idea that lessons exist in the past from which contemporary societies can benefit and learn. This idea, although controversial, has always been an intriguing one for historians. Those that agree that society can benefit from the past often quote philosopher George Santayana's famous statement, "Those who cannot remember the past are condemned to repeat it." Historians who ascribe to Santayana's philosophy believe that, for example, studying the events that led up to the major world wars or other significant historical events would allow society to chart a different and more favorable course in the future.

Just as difficult as convincing students to realize the importance of studying history is the search for useful and interesting supplementary materials that present historical events in a context that can be easily understood. The volumes in Lucent Books' World History Series attempt to present a broad, balanced, and penetrating view of the march of history. Ancient Egypt's important wars and rulers, for example, are presented against the rich and colorful backdrop of Egyptian religious, social, and cultural developments. The series engages the reader by enhancing historical events with these cultural contexts. For example, in *Ancient Greece*, the text covers the role of women in that society. Slavery is discussed in *The Roman Empire*, as well as how slaves earned their freedom. The numerous and varied aspects of everyday life in these and other societies are explored in each volume of the series. Additionally, the series covers the major political, cultural, and philosophical ideas as the torch of civilization is passed from ancient Mesopotamia and Egypt, through Greece, Rome, Medieval Europe, and other world cultures, to the modern day.

The material in the series is formatted in a thorough, precise, and organized manner. Each volume offers the reader a comprehensive and clearly written overview of an important historical event or period. The topic under discussion is placed in a broad historical context. For example, *The Italian Renaissance* begins with a discussion of the High Middle Ages and the loss of central control that allowed certain Italian cities to develop artistically. The book ends by looking forward to the Reformation and interpreting the societal changes that grew out of the Renaissance. Thus, students are not only involved in an historical era, but also enveloped by the events leading up to that era and the events following it.

One important and unique feature in the World History Series is the primary and secondary source quotations that richly supplement each volume. These quotes are useful in a number of ways. First, they allow students access to sources they would not normally be exposed to because of the difficulty and obscurity of the original source. The quotations range from interesting anecdotes to farsighted cultural perspectives and are drawn from historical witnesses both past and present. Second, the quotes demonstrate how and where historians themselves derive their information on the past as they strive to reach a consensus on historical events. Lastly, all of the quotes are footnoted, familiarizing students with the citation process and allowing them to verify quotes and/or look up the original source if the quote piques their interest.

Finally, the books in the World History Series provide a detailed launching point for further research. Each book contains a bibliography specifically geared toward student research. A second, annotated bibliography introduces students to all the sources the author consulted when compiling the book. A chronology of important dates gives students an overview, at a glance, of the topic covered. Where applicable, a glossary of terms is included.

In short, the series is designed not only to acquaint readers with the basics of history, but also to make them aware that their lives are a part of an ongoing human saga. Perhaps they will then come to the same realization as famed historian Arnold Toynbee. In his monumental work, *A Study of History*, he wrote about becoming aware of history flowing through him in a mighty current and of his own life "welling like a wave in the flow of this vast tide."

Important Dates in the History of the Reformation

1378	1390	1400	1410	1420	1430	1440	1450	1460	1470	1480	149●

1378–1417
Papal Schism: two popes reign at the same time in Rome, Italy, and Avignon, France

1414–1417
Council of Constance ends schism and condemns John Wycliffe (d. 1384) and Jan Hus, who is burned at the stake

1483
Martin Luther is born November 10

1484
Ulrich Zwingli is born January 1

1509
John Calvin is born; Henry VIII becomes king of England

1517
Luther publishes the Ninety-five Theses opposing sale of indulgences

1518
Luther appears before Cajetan in Augsburg

1519–1558
Reign of Charles V as Holy Roman Emperor

1520
Luther is excommunicated; Anabaptist movement begins

1521
Diet of Worms; Henry VIII writes *The Assertion of the Seven Sacraments Against Martin Luther;* is declared Defender of the Faith by Pope Leo X

1524
Peasants' revolt in Germany

1525
Capuchin order is founded; Zwingli stops saying Mass in Zurich and institutes new, simplified form of worship service emphasizing preaching

1527
Henry VIII begins annulment proceedings against his wife Catherine of Aragon

1529
Diet of Speyer; Lutheran princes mount first high-level protest (origin of word *Protestants*)

1530
Philipp Melanchthon publishes Augsburg Confession

1531
Schmalkaldic League is created; Zwingli is killed at battle of Kappel

1533
Henry marries Anne Boleyn; is excommunicated

1534
Act of Succession and Act of Supremacy in England; Ignatius of Loyola founds Society of Jesus

1535
Thomas More and Bishop John Fisher are executed in England; Ursuline order of nuns is founded in Italy

1536
Monasteries in England are dissolved; land is taken over by crown; first edition of Calvin's *Institutes of the Christian Religion* is published

1500 1510 1520 1530 1540 1550 1560 1570 1580 1590 1600 1610 1620

1541
Catholics and Protestants attempt to reconcile at Ratisbon

1542
Pope Paul III establishes Inquisition in Rome

1545–1563
Council of Trent

1546
Luther dies; John Knox comes to prominence in Scotland

1547
Chambre ardent created to try heretics in France; Henry VIII dies

1547–1553
Reign of Edward VI in England

1548
Loyola's *Spiritual Exercises* (written in 1521) is published

1554
Catholics' civil rights restored in England under Queen Mary

1555
Peace of Augsburg allows freedom of worship for Lutherans in some German provinces and for Catholics in others

1556
Loyola dies

1558
Protestantism is restored in England under Queen Elizabeth I

1558–1603
Reign of Elizabeth I in England

1559
John Knox returns to Scotland from exile in England and Switzerland

1560
Treaty of Edinburgh and Knox's Confession of Faith establish the Kirk of Scotland; Melanchthon dies

1563
Puritanism appears in England

1564
Calvin dies

1572
St. Bartholomew's Day Massacre of Protestants in France

1582
Spanish mystic Teresa of Ávila (b. 1515) dies

1593
Henry IV of France declares, "Paris is worth a Mass," and becomes Catholic to gain the throne

1598
Edict of Nantes grants freedom of worship in France

1620
Pilgrims (English separatists) leave Europe for North America

Introduction

From Medieval to Modern

In the first years of the sixteenth century, Europe was in the midst of great changes. Already voyages of discovery over the previous fifty years had opened up Africa, the Far East, and the Americas to European trade. The printing press had been invented and books were becoming more common; the artists and scholars of the Renaissance had opened up a new world of beauty and learning.

Revolutionary changes in the Western church, beginning in the early 1500s, further transformed European civilization. At that point nearly all of Europe was Christian and all Christians were Catholic. The Catholic Church was the center of everyone's life, from the poorest peasant to the king and his court. The celebration of holy days (holidays) marked the passing of the year. The church paid artists and architects to create monuments for the greater glory of God. The explorers and seafarers of the age of discovery sailed for gold, glory, and God. Indeed, the church had the final say on virtually all matters of importance. Even kings were expected to subject themselves to the laws of the church and to the pope, who was the head of the church. One of the most severe punishments for wrongdoing was excommunication, which meant being prohibited from receiving the sacraments, or

rites, of the church. Separation from the church meant separation from the whole community, so excommunication was a serious threat.

Of course, even during the Middle Ages, not every European was Christian.

A medieval woodcut depicts the torture of Jews. Despite persecution, followers of Judaism and other religions survived through the Middle Ages. The majority of Europe, however, adhered to the doctrines of the Catholic Church.

The sixteenth century was marked by religious and political upheaval as Europe attempted to reform the Catholic Church, which was seen as suffering from moral and theological abuses. A woodcut titled The Troubled Church in a Sea of Discontent *symbolizes the turbulence that characterized the Reformation.*

Judaism and Islam never completely disappeared from Europe, despite the effects of the Spanish Inquisition and the Crusades. However, there were so few Jews and Moslems in comparison to Christians that the average European of the fifteenth century had only a casual and probably distorted view of the beliefs of either religion.

In 1492 Ferdinand and Isabella of Spain made a serious effort to expel or convert all the Spanish Jews. Spain and the countries of eastern Europe also had sizable Moslem populations, which were not tolerated, either. In fact, stopping the spread of Islam into the rest of Europe was one of the few causes in which most European Christians, whatever their nationality, were united. Thousands of men, women, and children participated in the Crusades of the eleventh through the thirteenth

centuries in an effort to rid the world of Moslem "infidels."

The Reformation is the name given to the period in which the Christian community in Europe became fragmented. The Catholic Church continued to exist, but people called Protestants, who wanted to reform, or correct, the institutional church as it existed, went their separate ways. They started new varieties of the Christian religion, based upon the Bible and upon the life and teachings of Jesus of Nazareth, but differing from the Catholic Church and from one another in matters of belief and procedure.

Today it is sometimes hard to understand how the issues that drove the Reformation were so disruptive. Today most people tolerate religious diversity. In most parts of the world, people do not fight over the ideas fought about during the Reformation, such as the idea of salvation, or how many sacraments there are, or how to interpret a particular Bible passage, or which books actually belong in the Bible. But the world today is very different from the world in the early 1500s. Some people, including a number of kings and princes, liked the new Protestant ideas because they encouraged local authority instead of submission to the pope. Others liked the way some Protestants emphasized individualism and hard work. Still others found in Protestantism answers to questions about salvation and eternal life that they believed Catholicism had not provided.

What began as a religious movement had profound political and social implications as well. The Reformation changed Europe from an area united under one version of Christianity to a continent of separate nations, each with its own religious denomination and government. The Catholic Church headquartered in Rome was no longer the only accepted form of Christianity in Europe. Europe itself changed from a feudal to a commercial society. Its economy, which had been based on the hard work of peasants and farmers, became much more dependent on money and goods from commerce with other parts of the world. The Reformation was an integral part of the greater change that marked European civilization's move from the Middle Ages to modern times.

1 Europe on the Eve of Reformation

By 1500 most of Europe had been openly Christian for almost twelve hundred years. For three hundred years before that, Christians practiced their religion in secret, in fear of persecution from the Roman government. Then in A.D. 313 the emperor Constantine, who had converted to Christianity the year before, made it legal to practice that faith. The religion spread rapidly over the Middle East and Europe; indeed, for the period of the Middle Ages (about 500 to 1500), the history of Europe is to a large extent the history of the Catholic Church.

Church and State

As the Middle Ages drew to a close, there were no nations in the sense that the term is understood today. Throughout Europe groups of people who spoke the same language lived in traditional areas with borders that varied depending upon royal marriages, wars, and barbarian invasions. Germany, for example, was not a separate nation, but rather a collection of provinces, each headed by a king, a prince, a duke, or some other noble lord. All of the German lands, as well as parts of eastern Europe and, later, Spain, were part of the Holy Roman Empire, which was a loosely united alliance of Christian (hence "holy") territories. The "Roman" of the title signified a historical connection with the Roman Empire of the Caesars.

Some provinces of the Holy Roman Empire were more powerful than others, and their princes were called electors because they elected the new emperor. The empire's greatest rival was the kingdom of France, which had in turn an ongoing rivalry with the emerging power of England.

The emperor Constantine promoted the spread of Christianity when he made it a legal faith in the fourth century.

The advantage of the church in this political climate was that it was not defined by, and thus confined to, any land area. The pope, who was the head of the church, lived in Rome, but the church itself was everywhere. Priests and missionaries, who served the needs of the people anywhere they found them, reported to local bishops, who in turn reported to the pope. It was a simple but effective system. Because the priests, and especially the bishops, were often the best-educated people in any given area, people turned to them for nonspiritual as well as spiritual direction. Bishops often settled legal disputes, for example. Such willingness to submit to church authorities in civil matters was reinforced by the church's

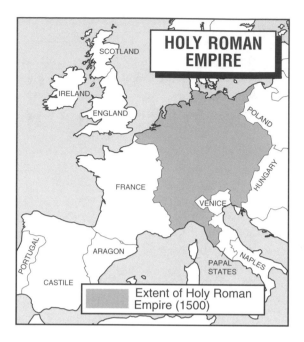

The papal court from a thirteenth-century woodcut (below). During this time, the papacy exercised great secular authority in Europe. Indeed, the church was the center of life and society.

The Church in the Middle Ages

Historian Will Durant, from his book The Reformation, *volume 6 of* The Story of Civilization, *describes the place of the church during the Middle Ages.*

"[The church] took the place vacated by the Roman Imperial government as the chief source of order and peace in the Dark Ages (approximately 524–1079 A.D.) of the Christian world. To the Church, more than to any other institution, Europe owed the resurrection of civilization in the West after the barbarian inundation of Italy, Gaul [France], Britain, and Spain. Her monks developed waste lands, her monasteries gave food to the poor, education to boys, lodging to travelers; her hospitals received the sick and destitute. Her nunneries sheltered mateless women and directed their maternal impulses to social ends; for centuries the nuns alone provided schooling for girls. If classic culture was not completely lost in the illiterate flood, it was because monks, while allowing or causing many pagan manuscripts to perish, copied and preserved thousands of them, and kept alive the Greek and Latin languages in which they were written. . . . For a thousand years . . . it was the Church that trained Western Europe's teachers, scholars, judges, diplomats, and ministers of state; the medieval state rested on the Church. When the Dark Ages ended . . . it was the Church that built the universities and the Gothic cathedrals, providing homes for the intellect, as well as for the piety, of men. . . . Through nine centuries almost all of European art was inspired and financed by the Church. . . .

Above all, the Church at her zenith gave to the states of Europe an international moral code and government. Just as the Latin language, taught in the schools by the Church, served as a unifying medium for the scholarship, literature, science, and philosophy of diverse nations, and just as the Catholic creed and ritual gave religious unity to a Europe not yet divided into sovereign nationalities, so the Roman Church . . . proposed herself as an international court, to which all rulers and states were to be morally responsible."

Priests (left) and bishops (right) not only provided spiritual guidance, but also often oversaw civil matters. For example, bishops often settled legal disputes.

practice of conferring a bishopric upon a member of the local, already powerful, nobility. Connections with the nobility were in turn good for the church because these wealthy families often contributed part of their landholdings to the church as payment for a bishop's appointment. Indeed, ultimately the practice of buying and selling church offices was one of the forms of corruption that Protestant reformers aimed to eliminate.

By about 1300 the church was the largest single landholder in Europe and had developed a complex and efficient financial system to deal with its income and expenses. In effect the church was a large state, or government, superimposed over all the smaller regional states of Europe. The church ran the schools, including the universities, and sponsored most of the art. Moreover, the church, as one historian puts it, "proposed herself as an international court, to which all rulers and states were to be morally responsible."[1]

Salvation

For the vast majority of Europeans in the Middle Ages, life centered around the church. In an age when people's lives were often cut short by accidents, by plague and other disease, by malnutrition, and by lack of medical knowledge, the concept of salvation was a matter of great practical concern. After this brief and possibly troubled life on earth, would one be saved, chosen to live forever in heaven with God? This was the promise of Christianity, but always the questions remained: How could one be sure? What did a person need to do to obtain this salvation?

The church offered many answers, but they boiled down to one: Follow the rules. The rules were the Ten Commandments and other orders and restrictions found in the Bible. In time the church added new rules and new interpretations to meet specific needs. The priest's job was to tell the people what the rules were and to give advice and instruction on how to follow them, live a Christian life, and thus ensure salvation. It is important to realize that in 1500 "the mass of the people of western Europe could neither read nor write—perhaps as many as two out of three were completely illiterate." The printing press had been around for about fifty years, but printed books were still a rarity—and very expensive. Thus most of what people knew about God and religion they learned by listening to the words of their priests. As historian Philip Hughes says, "It was by preaching that the converts were made, and upon preaching that the well-being of the Christian intelligence chiefly depended."[2]

The Expansion of the World

By 1500 the old ways were beginning to crumble. Big changes were afoot all over Europe, changes which would affect the church and every other aspect of life. Eu-

Beginning in the fifteenth and sixteenth centuries, a host of adventurers set out to explore the world. Here, Columbus reaches the New World, a pivotal event that led to great changes.

ropeans had to this point thought of the world as a fairly compact place, centered on the Mediterranean Sea (*medi* = middle; *terranean* = of the earth). But now explorers and adventurers were expanding the boundaries of the world. In the words of historian Harold J. Grimm:

> Now, within the span of a single life, such as that of Martin Luther (1483–1546), European seamen reached India and the Far East by sailing around Africa; discovered the two vast continents of North and South America and became familiar with their coasts from the Strait of Magellan to Labrador on the east and to Cape Mendocino on the west; circumnavigated the

globe, proving that the earth was round; and established a direct trade with the natives of the Far East and the New World.[3]

This expansion of the world had several effects. For one, it forced people to reevaluate their status in the world and consequently their relationship with God. For another, the increasing demand for trade in exotic foreign goods helped to organize a system of commerce and banking all over Europe, which stimulated the growth of cities and a whole new merchant class.

These new developments disrupted the entire medieval concept of society as a body, with the clergy as the head (moral and intellectual authority), the nobles as the arms (civil authority), and the peasants as the feet (labor). Where did the new townspeople—businessmen and artisans—fit? They were not nobles but some were quickly gaining social and political power through careful use of their new-found wealth. These townspeople, searching for their own place in society, would be among the first and strongest followers of the new Reformation churches.

Renaissance Humanism

Also at this time a new intellectual movement flourished, first in Italy, then all over Europe. This was the height of the Renaissance, when dogged and creative people in every field pushed the limits of what had been known and accepted. Scholars examined ancient Greek and Latin documents and reintroduced ideas and concepts that had been lost for centuries. They built on those ideas to express humanity's position in the new, expanding world. One group of scholars, known as Christian humanists, believed Christianity had gotten away from its authentic roots. They looked for original Hebrew and Greek texts of the Bible, as well as other works of early Christianity, hoping to use these primary source materials as a basis for reforming such objectionable church practices as simony (the selling of church offices), pluralism (bishops holding more than one office), and the toleration of corrupt and uneducated priests. As one historian says of the humanists, "They were above all distinguished by a belief in the power of the human intellect to bring about institutional and moral improvement."[4]

One of the most brilliant of Renaissance humanists, the Italian Giovanni Pico della Mirandola, expressed the view that the way to real learning and understand-

Increased trade spurred the development of commerce and banking (pictured), which, in turn, stimulated the growth of cities.

ing was to read and to question—not to limit oneself to one particular philosophy.

Those who have devoted themselves to any one of the schools of philosophy . . . can bring their doctrine into danger in the discussion of a few questions. But I have resolved not to swear by anyone's word, that I may base myself on all teachers of philosophy, examine all writings, recognize every school [of thought]. . . . Nor can anyone have selected rightly his own doctrine from all, unless he has first made himself familiar with all.[5]

This new independence of thought coincided with changing attitudes toward the clergy. The close connection between the nobility and the church leadership had bred corruption, as noble families who paid for bishoprics then expected preferential treatment. As early as the beginning of the fourteenth century, a cardinal, commenting on high church officials' lack of true concern for their followers, observed: "Nowadays, none of them [the bishops], or very few unhappily, are ever to be found leading their flocks to the pasture. What is to be noted is that all of them think only of shearing the sheep."[6]

The Papal Schism

Even the papacy, the church's highest office, suffered criticism and crises. Medieval and Renaissance popes often reached their position through influence exerted on their behalf by powerful nobles and rulers, such as Philip IV of France, who in 1307 arranged the election of a French pope. The king then persuaded the new pope to move his headquarters from Rome to Avignon, in France. For the next seventy years, called the Babylonian Captivity, a metaphorical reference to exile, the popes lived at Avignon, essentially puppets of the French ruling family.

Finally, in 1377 Pope Gregory XI returned the papacy to Rome, but he died shortly thereafter. His successor, Urban VI, "proved so violent of temper, and so insistent upon reforms uncongenial to the hierarchy" that the cardinals took another vote and declared his election invalid.[7] This time they chose a Frenchman, who again set up office in Avignon; but Urban, who was Italian, continued to act as pope in Rome. From 1378 to 1417 two popes claimed papal authority, and each area of Europe had to decide which was the "real" pope. The decision was more a matter of political alliances than religious belief. Each side declared that the other was not only wrong but heretical (against the true church). Each side declared that the other's priests could not properly administer the sacraments. This meant, among other things, that each side did not acknowledge baptisms and marriages performed by the opposing side.

By the 1390s everyone was pretty well fed up with the Papal Schism, as this dual papacy was called. Even some partisan cardinals were rethinking their positions, and eventually a group of them called for a general council. The tradition of church summit meetings, called councils, was an old one, based on the theory that a council was "the collected wisdom of all Christendom."[8] In 1409 a council met in the Italian city of Pisa, deposed both existing popes (neither of whom had showed up, despite being summoned), and elected a new one. Unfortunately, neither the

A papal commissioner issues indulgences at a German fair. The sale of indulgences was controversial: Many people denounced the practice as an attempt by a materialistic church to fill its coffers.

Avignon pope nor the pope in Rome recognized the council's authority, so now there were three popes.

The church muddled along for a few more years, until 1415, when another council was convened at Constance, on the German-Swiss border. This council had more clout, or perhaps the popes and cardinals were just worn out from all the fighting. In any case, the council deposed all three popes and elected a new one, Martin V. By 1417 everyone had accepted this compromise candidate and the schism was over, but at great cost to the prestige of the church in general and the papacy in particular. If even the popes acted from low motives—greed, desire for power, selfishness—how could anyone be expected to behave in a truly Christian manner?

Money and Indulgences

Always, popes and bishops needed to raise money. Running a large, multinational organization like the church was expensive from the start, and costs increased dramatically during the Late Middle Ages and the Renaissance. After all, this was the period in which some of the greatest painters, sculptors, architects, and builders in history created their finest works. Many of these masterpieces were paid for by the church. Additionally, the papacy maintained a standing army; protecting Rome from barbarians and other invaders was a costly operation.

To pay for all this grandeur and protection, the popes relied on funds collected from both the bishops and the people. In the first case, the popes imposed a variety of taxes on the bishops, who raised the money from their local kings and princes at every opportunity. Also, wealthy bishops paid high fees to hold more than one church office at a time. Such investments could be profitable, however, for the more areas they controlled, the more tax money they commanded.

To raise money from ordinary people, the church used other approaches. One method was to accept donations for indulgences, a practice that ultimately touched off the controversy that started the Reformation.

Indulgences were not new in the church. They were first offered during the Crusades in the 1100s, to encourage knights to make the difficult journey to the Holy Land and risk death fighting to free it from Moslem control. Whoever went on a Crusade was exempted from performing any penance that might otherwise have been imposed as punishment for past sins. The indulgence, or official excuse from performing acts of penance, was soon extended to anyone who financed a crusader; those who put up money got the same benefits as those who had gone themselves.

The indulgence was not intended to forgive sins nor to grant permission for the individual to go ahead and sin. "Indulgences always presupposed that a man's sins had been already forgiven, that he had turned from sin and was resolved to lead a new life."[9] However, a practice so vulnerable to abuse eventually got out of hand. Many people saw indulgences as something that the church never intended, namely, an easy pass to heaven. At the same time, the church found that indulgences brought in a significant amount of money.

Early Reformers

Two major "pre-Reformation reformers" deserve mention. The first was an Englishman, John Wycliffe (c. 1330–1384), a popular teacher and lecturer at prestigious Oxford University. Unimpressed with the character of the clergymen (priests and bishops) that served in his country, Wycliffe thought they were interested only in collecting money and living well. He also thought that the Papal Schism was scandalous and that people should "believe in popes only so far as these follow Christ." The vast majority of priests and bishops he bluntly called "robbers . . . malicious foxes . . . ravishing wolves . . . gluttons . . . devils . . . apes."[10]

Wycliffe believed that the church needed to completely separate itself from all its possessions and power. To this point, he was only suggesting a return to the ideals of Jesus and the apostles. But Wycliffe went further, holding opinions about the sacraments that went strongly against those held by the church. He disapproved, for example, of the practice of confessing out loud to a priest; he wanted instead a return to the earlier practice of voluntary public confession. More signifi-

Wycliffe's Propositions

Some of John Wycliffe's propositions, which were condemned by the church in 1382, are excerpted here from Henry Bettenson's Documents of the Christian Church.

"3. That Christ is not in the sacrament [of eucharist] essentially and really, in his own corporeal [bodily] presence.

4. That it is not laid down in the Gospel that Christ ordained the Mass. . . .

7. That if a man be duly penitent any outward confession is superfluous and useless. . . .

14. That any deacon or priest may preach the word of God apart from the authority of the Apostolic See [the pope's office] or a Catholic bishop. . . .

17. That the people can at their own will correct sinful lords. . . .

35. That the Roman Church is the synagogue of Satan, and the Pope is not the next and immediate vicar of Christ and the Apostles."

In the 1300s, English religious reformer John Wycliffe voiced opinions contrary to the church. His ideas would become important during the Reformation.

cantly, however, he disagreed with the church's teaching about the sacrament of communion. The church taught that during the Mass the priest changed the bread and wine into the body and blood of Jesus. Wycliffe believed that Jesus was somehow (he did not know how) present in the bread and wine, but denied that the sacramental elements underwent physical transformation.

Wycliffe also believed that people were saved not by acts performed in their lifetime but because their salvation had been preordained by God. He preached that

Influenced by Wycliffe, Jan Hus was a staunch advocate of church reform. Hus was burned at the stake for his heretical views.

the Bible should be available in translations anyone could read: If people had direct access to the guide to religion, they would be less dependent upon the church. And he believed that governments should not be subordinate to the church. Though in the 1300s Wycliffe's ideas had only a small impact, all would become important more than 150 years later during the Reformation.

Another early reformer was Jan Hus, who lived and preached in Prague, long a center of culture and trade in medieval Europe. He had read some of Wycliffe's sermons and letters and agreed with most of what the English reformer believed. Like so many others unhappy with the Papal Schism, Hus argued for church reform, declaring: "To rebel against an erring pope is to obey Christ."[11]

In 1415 bishops at the Council of Constance (the same council that ended the Papal Schism) condemned the works of both Wycliffe and Hus. The council undoubtedly wished to compensate for the confusion that had reigned in the church during the schism by making a strong statement of authority. Although Wycliffe had died in 1384, Jan Hus was very much alive. The council seized Hus, who had been invited to attend under a guaranty of safe conduct, ordered his writings burned, and turned him over to the local authorities, who found Hus guilty of heresy and burned him at the stake.

Wycliffe and Hus were men ahead of their time. A century after Hus was burned, others proclaimed almost the same ideas, and this time their words took hold all over Europe.

Chapter

2 "I Cannot Do Otherwise": Martin Luther

Before the autumn of 1517 Martin Luther was no one of importance outside his university community in Wittenberg, a small town in the remote German province of Saxony. Within a few months, however, Luther would be known throughout the German lands, and within three years his

Martin Luther's clarion call for church reform touched off the controversy that led to the Reformation.

name would be attached to a religious and social movement that would change the history of the world.

Martin Luther was born on November 10, 1483, St. Martin's Day. His parents were able to send him to good schools, and he attended the university at Erfurt. He began a study of law to please his father, but abandoned it in 1505 to become an Augustinian monk. He took his life in this mendicant order very seriously and worked hard at it. As he once said:

> I was a pious monk, and so strictly observed the rules of my order that . . . if ever a monk got into heaven by monkery, so should I also have gotten there. . . . If it had lasted longer I should have tortured myself to death with watching, praying, reading, and other work.[12]

Luther progressed rapidly as a monk, was ordained as a priest, and soon had a position teaching classes on the Bible at the University of Wittenberg. According to one student, Professor Luther was a good lecturer, with a voice that was easy to listen to, and "he spoke neither too quickly nor too slowly, but at an even pace, without hesitation and very clearly, and in such fitting order that every part flowed naturally out of what went before."[13]

Justification by Faith

Luther, like so many other people of his time, worried about being saved. But perhaps more than most, he felt unworthy, unloved, and unforgiven no matter what he did. Not even becoming a monk helped:

> When I was a monk I used . . . to believe that it was all over with my salvation every time I experienced the concupiscence of the flesh, that is to say an evil movement against one of the brethren [his fellow monks], of envy, of anger, or hatred, or of jealousy and so forth. I used to try various remedies; I used to go to confession every day, but that didn't help me at all. For . . . I could never find peace, but was everlastingly tormented.[14]

Because of these feelings of unworthiness, Luther looked for ways to be sure of salvation, but he was never happy with the ways the church already offered. As one historian puts it, "The Catholic Church had, in his judgment, too low an opinion of the majesty and holiness of God and too high an estimate of the worth and potentiality of man."[15] In other words, Luther thought that God was far too high and holy ever to be approached by low, sinful humans like himself, no matter how many good works they did.

Luther finally found the guidance he needed in the Bible. In one of the books of the New Testament, the Epistle (letter) to the Romans, he read, "The just shall live by faith."[16] To Luther that meant that no amount of good works could ever bring a person to salvation; only faith would do that. God freely gives people

To finance the rebuilding of St. Peter's, Pope Leo X authorized the sale of indulgences, an event that would prove pivotal in Luther's break with the Catholic Church.

love and mercy: his grace. For Luther, coming to the belief that grace cannot be earned was a great relief. He no longer had to worry about doing penance for his sins—he had only to have faith. This understanding of salvation is known by the phrase "justification by faith."

As he studied and thought, Luther began to develop for himself some of the ideas that would later cause him great trouble with the Catholic Church. At the time he considered himself—and was—a good Catholic. His first steps into controversy and separation from the church began in November 1517, when Pope Leo X authorized the offering of an indulgence in the neighboring territory of Mainz.

Johann Tetzel was an engaging speaker authorized to preach indulgences. People came from all over to offer money in exchange for indulgences.

Pope Leo's Indulgence

Pope Leo needed to finance the rebuilding of the monumental basilica of St. Peter's in Rome. Albert of Brandenburg, a young German nobleman who also held multiple archbishoprics, was seriously behind in payment of taxes to the pope. So the pope offered a deal: He would allow Albert to authorize an indulgence in Mainz for eight years if Albert would send half of the money collected to the pope. Albert readily agreed.

A typical way to offer indulgences was to "preach" them. This meant that a popular and eloquent speaker would travel the countryside, holding public services somewhat like revival meetings or parish missions at churches in the region. Such events were announced ahead of time, and people came from all over to hear the preacher and to offer their money in ex-

change for indulgences. Albert authorized one of the best known and most popular of local preachers, Johann Tetzel, to organize the preaching of the 1517 indulgence. Tetzel was a Dominican and had made a name for himself as a talented preacher.

According to a Franciscan friar who witnessed some of Tetzel's missions:

This indulgence was highly respected. When the commissioner [preacher] was welcomed to town, the papal bull [letter from the pope authorizing the indulgence] was carried on velvet or gold cloth. All the priests, monks, councilmen, teachers, pupils, men, women, maids, and children went to meet him singing in solemn procession with flags and candles. The bells tolled and when he entered the church the organ played. A red cross was put up in the middle of the church to which the Pope's banner was affixed. In short: even God himself could not have been welcomed and received more beautifully.[17]

Once in town, Tetzel announced the availability of the indulgence to all who would confess their sins and contribute as much as they were able to the rebuilding of St. Peter's. He told these people that their sins were forgiven and that they would no longer be held responsible for "all punishment which you deserve in purgatory . . . so that when you die the gates of punishment shall be shut, and the gates of the paradise of delight shall be opened."[18]

This was of course just what most people wanted to hear. They could confess their sins, donate some money, and go directly to heaven. It would no longer be necessary to worry about hell or about purgatory, the spiritual "waiting room" where, according to Catholic doctrine, the souls of the dead did additional penance before being admitted to heaven. There are numerous reports that Tetzel extended his mandate to allow people to buy indulgences for souls already in purgatory.

Not everyone was convinced of the validity of Tetzel's claims: Surely it was a skeptic who came up with the often-repeated rhyme, "When coin in coffer rings, the soul from purgatory springs." Another critic reported:

> It is incredible what this ignorant monk said and preached. He gave sealed letters stating that even the sins which a man was intending to commit would be forgiven. The pope, he said, had more power than all the Apostles, all the angels and saints, more even than the Virgin Mary herself; for these were all subject to Christ [Jesus], but the pope was equal to Christ.[19]

It is unlikely that Tetzel actually claimed any such thing. As one historian comments, "He was an enthusiastic salesman, but not quite conscienceless."[20] Tetzel was probably overstating and oversimplifying his case to such an extent that many common people believed the exaggerated claims.

Elector Frederick of Saxony had not allowed Tetzel to preach the St. Peter's indulgence within the borders of Saxony. Frederick preferred to keep his subjects' money at home, where he could use it for his own causes. But during the missions in Mainz, Tetzel came so close to Frederick's borders that many Saxons crossed over to hear the monk preach and to offer their money.

In exchange for their contributions, penitents received a letter announcing the terms of the indulgence. Several citizens of Wittenberg returned with their letters and brought them to the learned Professor Luther, asking him to verify that the claims were true. Luther could not in conscience do this, and when Tetzel heard of Luther's refusal, he struck back by criticizing Luther.

The Ninety-Five Theses

Perhaps Tetzel thought that Luther would back down in the face of criticism from the popular and well-known preacher, but he did not know Luther. Writing in Latin, Luther proceeded to set down ninety-five theses, or arguments, in which he attempted to clarify the theology of indulgences. He called the document *Disputatio pro declaratione virtutis indulgentiarum (Disputation for Clarification of the Power of Indulgences)*. This famous document has

Luther Sends His Theses to Albert of Brandenburg

On October 31, 1517, Luther posted his Ninety-five Theses at Wittenberg. On the same day, he sent a copy to Albert of Brandenburg. This excerpt from the covering letter appears in volume 48 of Luther's Works.

"Forgive me that I, the least of all men, have the temerity [boldness] to consider writing to Your Highness. . . . Under your most distinguished name, papal indulgences are offered all across the land for the construction of St. Peter. Now, I do not so much complain about the quacking of the preachers, which I haven't heard; but I bewail the gross misunderstanding among the people which comes from these preachers and which they spread everywhere among common men. Evidently the poor souls believe that when they have bought indulgence letters they are then assured of their salvation. They are likewise convinced that souls escape from purgatory as soon as they have placed a contribution into the chest. . . .

O great God! The souls committed to your care, excellent Father, are thus directed to death. For all these souls you have the heaviest and a constantly increasing responsibility. Therefore I can no longer be silent on this subject. . . . After all, the indulgences contribute absolutely nothing to the salvation and holiness of souls; they only compensate for the external punishment which—on the basis of Canon Law—once used to be imposed. . . .

I can only beg you, Most Reverend Father, through the Lord Jesus Christ, to deign to give this matter your fatherly attention . . . and command the preachers of indulgences to preach in another way. . . .

Were it agreeable to you, Most Reverend Father, you could examine my disputation theses, so that you may see how dubious is this belief concerning indulgences, which these preachers propagate as if it were the surest thing in the whole world."

been known ever since as the Ninety-five Theses.

According to tradition Luther posted a copy of the Ninety-five Theses on the church door at Wittenberg at noon on October 31, 1517. A huge crowd was expected the following day for the Feast of All Saints, and the church door was a kind of public bulletin board. It makes a dramatic scene—Luther hammering his paper against the large wooden doors—but it probably never happened. Luther wrote extensively about his life and about his career and theses, and he never mentioned a public posting of the theses. He says only:

> Then I wrote a letter with the Theses to the bishop of Magdeburg, admonishing and beseeching him to stop Tetzel and prevent this stupid thing from being preached. . . . So my theses against Tetzel's articles, which you can now see in print, were published. They went throughout the whole of Germany in a fortnight.[21]

The story of the church door was probably started a few years after Luther's death by one of his followers. Because it is plausible enough and has great appeal, it has become accepted.

The Ninety-five Theses were statements about Luther's interpretation of the church's teaching on indulgences. Among other things, Luther says clearly that the pope has no ability to do away with "any penalties except those imposed by his own authority," and that any "who believe that they can be certain of their salvation because they have indulgence letters will be eternally damned." Another thesis states that "Christians are to be taught that he who gives to the poor or lends to the needy does a better deed than he who buys indulgences."[22]

By today's standards there is nothing radical about these statements. But Luther's vocal protest at the way indulgences were preached and used struck a chord with many discontented Catholics. All over Europe people talked and wrote about the theses. A war of words began, taking Luther down a road from which he could not turn back.

Luther Against the Pope

The more Luther wrote in response to his critics, the more specific and the more hardened his complaints became. By April 1518 he had rejected not only the indulgence preached by Tetzel, but all the recent practices of the popes in selling indulgences. He further asserted that a council of bishops had greater authority

A rather fanciful illustration shows Luther posting his Ninety-five Theses on the church door at Wittenberg. His forceful theses, or propositions, questioned the church's practice of issuing indulgences.

The Ninety-Five Theses

There was no formal debate on Luther's Ninety-five Theses on indulgences. However, their contents were spread both by word of mouth and by printed copies, and many people discussed them in print for years to come. This partial list is from volume 31 of Luther's Works.

"Out of love and zeal for truth and the desire to bring it to light, the following theses will be publicly discussed at Wittenberg under the chairmanship of the reverend father Martin Luther, Master of Arts and Sacred Theology and regularly appointed Lecturer on these subjects at that place. He requests that those who cannot be present to debate orally with us will do so by letter.

1. When our Lord and Master Jesus Christ said, 'Repent,' he willed the entire life of believers to be one of repentance.
2. This word cannot be understood as referring to the sacrament of penance, that is, confession and satisfaction, as administered by the clergy.
3. Yet it does not mean solely inner repentance; such inner repentance is worthless unless it produces various outward mortifications of the flesh. . . .
5. The pope neither desires nor is able to remit [do away with] any penalties except those imposed by his own authority or that of the canons [the laws of the church]. . . .
32. Those who believe that they can be certain of their salvation because they have indulgence letters will be eternally damned, together with their teachers. . . .
37. Any true Christian, whether living or dead, participates in all the blessings of Christ and the church; and this is granted him by God, even without indulgence letters. . . .
41. Papal indulgences must be preached with caution, lest people erroneously think that they are preferable to other good works of love. . . .
43. Christians are to be taught that he who gives to the poor or lends to the needy does a better deed than he who buys indulgences. . . .
48. Christians are to be taught that the pope, in granting indulgences, needs and thus desires their devout prayer more than their money."

than the pope. Pope Leo X, still struggling to finance St. Peter's, as well as other artistic and military activities, grew angry at Luther and summoned the annoying monk to Rome.

Luther was reluctant to obey, fearing that the pope, his "boss," would banish him to an obscure monastery or silence him in some other way. He protested the pope's summons through his friend George Spalatin, the chaplain to Elector Frederick of Saxony. In response, Pope Leo agreed to let Luther be questioned instead at Augsburg, in Germany, where soon an imperial diet (council) was to meet. Representing the pope there would be Cardinal Tommaso di Vio, known as Cajetan.

In October 1518, not quite a year after the publication of the Ninety-five Theses, Luther appeared before Cajetan at Augsburg. Luther had hoped for a chance to explain his views to someone with power and influence in the church. Cajetan, however, focused on the issue of authority: A monk, who vows obedience to his superiors, should not be allowed to criticize them publicly. The meeting satisfied neither man, and Luther returned to Wittenberg angrier than ever.

The Growing Challenge

After his meeting with Cajetan, Luther began referring to the pope as the Antichrist and urging that "a common reformation should be undertaken" of both spiritual and worldly matters.[23] In June 1520 he wrote to Spalatin:

> I have cast the die. . . . I will not reconcile myself to them [the Roman church] for all eternity. . . . Let them condemn and burn all that belongs to me; in return I will do as much for them. . . . Now I no longer fear, and I am publishing a book in the German tongue about Christian reform, directed against the pope, in language as violent as if I were addressing the Antichrist.[24]

Up to this point all of Luther's writings had been in Latin, intended for an audience primarily of other scholars. Now he began to write pamphlets in German as well, and with the aid of the printing press these pamphlets were spread over all German-speaking lands. Three pamphlets written in 1520—*An Open Letter to the Christian Nobility of the German Nation Concerning the Reform of the Christian Estate, The Babylonian Captivity of the Church,* and *The Freedom of a Christian*—were tracts not only of religious reform but also of national pride and honor.

In *An Open Letter to the Christian Nobility* Luther says, "Now that Italy is sucked dry, the Romanists are coming into Germany. . . . How is it that we Germans must put up with such robbery and extortion of our goods at the hands of the pope?"[25] In addition to calling on Germans to join a revolt against the church for economic reasons, this pamphlet also claimed that *all* Christians were members of the priesthood, and that the idea of ordained priests as a separate category was unnecessary. The pamphlet sold out its first printing of four thousand copies in less than three weeks.

In *The Babylonian Captivity,* Luther compared the church's "captivity" by Rome to the time over two thousand years earlier when the Jews had been forced to leave Israel to become prisoners in Babylon. He claimed that the popes held the church in captivity by deceiving the people about the meaning and purpose of the holy sacraments, the religious rituals Christians believe to have been established by Jesus. "In the first place," writes Luther, "I must deny that there are seven sacraments, and must for the present maintain that there are only three, baptism, penance, and the bread [communion]."[26] In later years he would recognize only two, baptism and communion. In either case, rejecting the other sacraments (confirmation, marriage, holy orders, and anointing the sick) was a startling and very important departure from Catholic doctrine.

In the third pamphlet, *The Freedom of a Christian*, Luther says that "a Christian is free from all things and over all things so that he needs no works to make him righteous and save him, since faith alone abundantly confers all these things."[27] The question of whether good works contributed to salvation or whether faith alone was relevant would be debated by the reformers for years.

Luther's Excommunication

In June 1520 Pope Leo issued a bull, or papal letter, that was a ringing condemnation of certain of Luther's statements. Leo began by listing the "mischievous" ideas and troublesome errors in doctrine that were circulating at the time in parts of Germany. He went on:

Moreover, since the aforesaid errors, and many others, are contained in var-

ious writings of Martin Luther . . . we [the pope, speaking officially] likewise condemn whatever he has written . . . and forbid the faithful of Christ to read [his writings], to praise, print, publish or defend them.[28]

The pope then gave Luther sixty days to recant, or take back, his statements. If he failed to do so, he would be excommunicated, or prohibited from partaking of the sacraments of the church.

By this time, however, Luther was committed to reform. Many scholars and others supported his statements, and he took that to mean that God wanted him to continue to fight against the pope. Now he stated flatly that the church, as it currently existed, was the "most lawless den of robbers, the most shameless of all brothels, the very kingdom of sin, death, and hell."[29] When Luther learned that representatives of the pope were burning copies of his pamphlets, he responded dramatically. At the end of his sixty-day grace period, he gathered a group of university students and professors for a large bonfire, throwing in copies of church laws and books that supported the papacy. Luther then added a copy of *Exsurge Domine*, the bull that condemned him. The next day he proclaimed that no one who submitted to the rule of the pope could be saved. As historian Will Durant puts it, "The monk had excommunicated the pope."[30]

Despite this clear break with papal authority, Luther's struggles with secular authority were yet to come. Luther had hoped that the new Holy Roman Emperor, Charles V, would help lead a reform movement in the church. Charles was not opposed to limiting papal power in his do-

In a dramatic move against papal authority, Luther burns Exsurge Domine, *the bull that threatened to excommunicate him.*

mains, but he remained loyal to his coronation oath to defend the church. Nevertheless, he could not ignore the uproar reformers had caused in the German provinces. Many people, including some of the electors, felt strongly that Luther was right when he said that the pope had far too much power over them. In particular, Elector Frederick of Saxony was a staunch defender of Luther. Charles decided to hear what Luther had to say, and summoned him to an imperial diet scheduled to be held in the city of Worms in April 1521.

Luther was delighted to accept the summons, as he welcomed any opportunity to express his views. He drew large crowds everywhere he spoke, and every speech gave him more confidence in the rightness of what he was doing. Crowds followed his carriage to Worms. When he was warned that there might be dangers ahead, Luther told his friend Spalatin that

he would go to Worms even if there were "as many devils in it as there were tiles of the roofs of the houses."[31]

The Diet of Worms

Luther appeared before the emperor at the Diet of Worms; there he was asked, "Do you wish to defend all your acknowledged books, or to retract some?" Luther confirmed that the books under discussion were certainly his, unless they had somehow been changed during the publication process, then asked the assembly to note that "my books are not all of the same kind. For there are some in which I have discussed religious faith and morals simply . . . so that even my enemies themselves are compelled to admit that these are useful, harmless, and clearly worthy to be read by Christians." He continued:

*Luther at the Diet of Worms, where he was asked to recant his "heretical"
religious views.*

Another group of my books attacks
the papacy and the affairs of the papists as those who both by their doctrines and very wicked examples have
laid waste the Christian world with evil
that affects the spirit and the body. . . .
Also, property and possessions, especially in this illustrious nation of Germany, have been devoured by an
unbelievable tyranny. . . . If, therefore,
I should have retracted these writings,
I should have done nothing other
than to have added strength to this
[papal] tyranny and I should have
opened not only windows but doors to
such great godlessness.[32]

Luther went on to say that he would
be happy if the emperor or anyone else
could show him any errors in his teachings, but that he was delighted "to see excitement and dissension arise because of
the Word of God." When he had finished
his speech, the emperor again asked for a
simple answer: Did Luther or did he not
wish to retract his books? Luther replied:

> Unless I am convinced by the testi-
> mony of the scriptures or by clear rea-
> son (for I do not trust either in the
> pope or in councils alone, since it is
> well known that they have often erred
> and contradicted themselves), I am
> bound by the Scriptures I have quoted
> and my conscience is captive to the
> word of God. I cannot and I will not
> retract anything, since it is neither safe
> nor right to go against conscience.[33]

Luther's most famous declaration may
not have been spoken at the end of these

Luther at the Diet of Worms

Martin Luther's Works *are available in English in a fifty-five-volume set published under the general editorship of Helmut T. Lehmann. These excerpts from Luther's speech before the emperor Charles and the German princes at Worms on April 18, 1521, appear in volume 32.*

"Most serene emperor, most illustrious princes, concerning those questions proposed to me yesterday on behalf of your serene majesty, whether I acknowledged as mine the books enumerated and published in my name and whether I wished to persevere in their defense or to retract them, I have given to the first question my full and complete answer, in which I still persist and shall persist forever. These books are mine and they have been published in my name by me.

In replying to the second question, I ask that [you] note that my books are not all of the same kind. For there are some in which I have discussed religious faith and morals simply . . . so that even my enemies themselves are compelled to admit that these are useful, harmless, and clearly worthy to be read by Christians. . . .

Another group of my books attacks the papacy and the affairs of the papists as those who both by their doctrines and very wicked examples have laid waste the Christian world with evil that affects the spirit and the body. . . . If, therefore, I should have retracted these writings, I should have done nothing other than to have added strength to this tyranny and I should have opened not only windows but doors to such great godlessness. . . .

I have written a third sort of book against some private and (as they say) distinguished individuals—those, namely, who strive to preserve the Roman tyranny and to destroy the godliness taught by me. Against these I confess I have been more violent than my religion or profession demands. But then, I do not set myself up as a saint; neither am I disputing about my life, but about the teaching of Christ. It is not proper for me to retract these works, because by this retraction it would again happen that tyranny and godlessness would, with my patronage, rule and rage among the people of God more violently than ever before."

Luther on Men, Women, and Marriage

Luther had an opinion on every subject. Here, in this excerpt from his essay on marriage, found in volume 45 of his Works, *he discusses the roles of men and women.*

"This is also how to comfort and encourage a woman in the pangs of childbirth . . . [say] remember that you are a woman, and that this work of God in you is pleasing to him. Trust joyfully in his will, and let him have his way with you. Work with all your might to bring forth the child. Should it mean your death, then depart happily, for you will die in a noble deed and in subservience to God. If you were not a woman you should now wish to be one for the sake of this very work alone, that you might thus gloriously suffer and even die in the performance of God's work and will.

Now you tell me, when a father goes ahead and washes diapers or performs some other mean task for his child, and someone ridicules him as an effeminate fool—though that father is acting in the spirit just described and in Christian faith—my dear fellow you tell me, which of the two is most keenly ridiculing the other? God, with all his angels and creatures, is smiling—not because that father is washing diapers, but because he is doing so in Christian faith. Those who sneer at him and see only the task but not the faith are ridiculing God with all his creatures, as the biggest fool on earth. Indeed, they are only ridiculing themselves."

words, but only added later to written copies of his statement, but the words nevertheless express his feelings at the time: "I cannot do otherwise, here I stand, may God help me, Amen."[34]

This definite and dramatic answer did not please the emperor. He responded:

And after having heard the obstinate answer which Luther gave yesterday, April 18, in the presence of us all, I declare to you that I regret having so long delayed to proceed against this Luther and his false doctrine and I am no longer willing to hear him speak more, but I am making it clear that immediately . . . he be taken back . . . without preaching or admonishing the people with his bad doctrine. . . . I am determined to proceed against him as a notorious heretic.[35]

Luther later wrote to a friend that he was disappointed yet again at the loss of an opportunity to argue his beliefs with learned theologians.

> I thought his Imperial Majesty would have assembled one or fifty scholars and overcome this monk in a straightforward manner. But nothing else was done there than this: Are these your books? Yes. Do you want to renounce them or not? No. Then go away![36]

Luther as Outlaw

The emperor's edict was the final blow separating Luther from all that had gone before. The pope had excommunicated him from the church; now the emperor outlawed him from society. On his way home to Wittenberg, Luther had an interview with his longtime supporter, Elector Frederick, now obligated to follow the emperor's edict. With Luther's consent Frederick arranged to have Luther "captured"

on his way home and taken to a safe place, at Wartburg Castle. There Luther stayed for the next ten months, writing, studying, fine-tuning his theological ideas, and recording one of his greatest achievements, the first translation of the New Testament into German.

Following Luther's condemnation by the Edict of Worms, Elector Frederick—who defended Luther's views—arranged to have the excommunicated monk "abducted" and taken to Wartburg Castle (bottom). (Top) In this isolated chamber at Wartburg, Luther spent ten months translating the New Testament into German.

Even Luther's views on marriage conflicted with the church. Years after he formulated these views, Luther himself would marry, in a departure from Catholic dogma.

Luther believed that people came to faith by reading and understanding the Bible, and he always emphasized the central role of Scripture in the life of a Christian. His understanding of the Bible led to his belief in fewer sacraments, and to an interpretation of communion fundamentally different from that of the church. For one thing, a long-standing tradition in the church dictated that only the priests took both bread and wine at communion; the people received bread only. Luther came to believe that all people should receive both.

More significant, however, was Luther's understanding of the meaning of communion. For centuries theologians had discussed and debated the issue, finally settling upon an explanation that said that the bread and wine actually changed into the body and blood of Jesus during the celebration of the Mass. The appearance was still that of bread and wine, but the substance was that of Jesus. That this could happen, invisible to human eyes, was considered the great mystery of faith.

Luther believed that Jesus was somehow present along with the substance of the bread and wine. That is, the bread was Jesus but it was also still bread. Luther also rejected the belief that every time the Mass was celebrated, Jesus' sacrifice—that is, his death on the cross to redeem the sins of all people—was made again. He did not believe that the Mass itself was a sacrifice, only that it helped worshipers remember the sacrifice of the Crucifixion.

In another departure from dogma, Luther also believed that there was no support in the Bible for the dictum that priests and monks remain unmarried, and he encouraged young monks to leave their monasteries and marry.

By this time, four years after the Ninety-five Theses, Luther's ideas were already strongly entrenched in Germany and elsewhere. The fact that Luther had defied the emperor at Worms, and had lived to tell the tale, encouraged his followers. Luther maintained a huge correspondence with his friends, and they carried on with reform despite his absence. There was no turning back from a major change in the practice of Christianity in Europe.

Why Luther?

Why did such dramatic changes follow upon the words of Martin Luther? Others, like Wycliffe and Hus in the 1300s and 1400s, had said many of the same things, but never before had their ideas caught on to any great degree. If ever a person was in the right place at the right time, Martin Luther was. The German people of the sixteenth century prized individualism. They were more than willing to listen to a man who spoke to them about freeing themselves from the authority of a foreign prince (the pope). Luther spoke to them eloquently, and in their common language, about taking charge of their spiritual lives and becoming their own interpreters of the Bible. In simplified form, this philosophy has often been expressed as "Every man his own priest." Luther's strength of belief, his ability with words, and his forceful personality seem to have been the factors that catalyzed change. The Reformation had begun—but it had a long way to go.

3 The King's "Great Matter": Reformation in England

In England, reformation took a different turn. Many English intellectuals agreed with at least some of the ideas of Martin Luther, but the majority of the people, who could not read Latin or German, were relatively unaffected by the pronouncements coming from Wittenberg. Instead, the decision to break from the hierarchy of the Catholic Church was made by one man, almost entirely on personal and political grounds. The issue was simple: Who was to be in charge of the English church, the pope or the king?

King Henry VIII, one of the most famous kings of all time, was an intelligent and energetic man, well loved by his subjects. In his prime, he was handsome and athletic. And he desperately wanted a male heir. He was convinced that without a son to follow him, England would be plunged into war. In Henry's mind, not only was the continuation of his own bloodline at stake, so was "the quiet (or the ruin) of our kingdom."[37]

Henry was eighteen years old when he married Catherine of Aragon. The royal couple had one daughter, Mary. Catherine bore other children, including several sons, but none lived longer than a few weeks. In 1527, having been married for half his life, Henry concluded that Catherine would never have a son who survived

King Henry VIII's demand to control the English church fueled reformation in England.

to adulthood, and he thought he should marry a woman who would be able to have healthy sons. He even had the woman in mind: Anne Boleyn, a lady-in-waiting and the niece of the duke of Norfolk.

Henry VIII, along with nearly everyone else in the Christian world, believed that a marriage between two baptized people could never be dissolved: The marriage was inviolable until one of the spouses died. Accordingly, he did not seek to divorce Catherine in the sense that people understand divorce today. Instead he hoped to obtain from the church an official acknowledgment that his marriage to Catherine had never been valid in the first place, and therefore he was free to remarry. Such an official acknowledgment is called an annulment.

Henry based his case for annulment on the undisputed fact that twenty-five years earlier Catherine had been married to his older brother, Arthur. This marriage between two teenagers had been arranged by Arthur and Henry's father, Henry VII, and Catherine's parents, Ferdinand and Isabella of Spain. Arthur died only a few months after the wedding. Since young Henry (twelve years old at the time) was next in line to be king, the two sets of parents arranged for Catherine to marry Henry to assure continued "peace and friendship [between England and Spain]."[38]

Before the formal wedding, Henry and Catherine obtained from Pope Julius II a dispensation, or special permission, to marry. This was necessary because there were rules about marrying relatives, and Catherine was Henry's sister-in-law. At the time, Henry and nearly everyone else considered the dispensation a mere formality.

Now, after eighteen years of marriage, Henry wanted the new pope, Clement VII, to say that Julius had been wrong. He wanted an official statement that he and Catherine had never been legally married. In effect he wanted a dispensation from the dispensation.

The King's Conscience

Henry's first step was to ask for help from Cardinal Thomas Wolsey, the archbishop of York and lord chancellor of England. After the king, Cardinal Wolsey was the most powerful man in England. However, while most English people loved their

Seeking an annulment, Henry VIII solicited the help of Cardinal Thomas Wolsey (pictured), the politically powerful but much despised lord chancellor of England.

How to Advise a King

The title of Thomas More's Utopia *means "nowhere," although the word has come to mean a place that is perfect and good. In this selection from the book, written in 1515, More and his friend Peter are talking to Raphael, who has traveled widely. They suggest that he become an adviser to a king, but Raphael calls it "slavery."*

"Peter replied, 'I do not mean that you should be a slave to any king, only that you should be of service to him.'

'The difference is a mere matter of words,' Raphael replied. . . . 'Imagine me at the court of the King of France. Suppose I were sitting in his council with the King himself presiding. . . . Suppose the councillors are discussing how they can raise money for the King's treasury. . . . All the councillors agree: a king can never have enough money, since he has to maintain his army; a king can do nothing unjustly even if he wants to; all property belongs to the king, even the very persons of his subjects; no man has any other property than what the king out of his goodness thinks fit to leave him; the king should leave him as little as possible, as if it were to his advantage that his people should have neither riches nor liberty. For wealth and freedom make men less submissive to a cruel and unjust rule, whereas poverty dulls them, makes them patient, and bears down and breaks that spirit which might otherwise dispose them to rebel.

'Now what if after this advice was given, I should get up and assert that such counsel was both dishonorable and ruinous to a king? And that both his honor and his safety consisted more in his people's wealth than in his own. . . . If I would press these views on men strongly inclined to the contrary, how deaf they would be to it all!'

'Stone deaf, no doubt,' I [Thomas More] said, 'and no wonder! To tell the truth, it seems to me that you should not offer advice which you know will not be considered. What good could it do?'"

king, they despised Wolsey. He was vain and extravagant and boastful and he did much of the king's dirty work, such as imposing taxes. Sometimes he even seemed to forget who was actually king. According to one foreign observer:

On my first arrival in England, the Cardinal used to say to me, "His Majesty will do so and so." Subsequently, by degrees, he forgot himself, and commenced saying, "We shall do so and so." At present he . . . says, "I shall do so and so." . . . If it were necessary to neglect either King or Cardinal, it would be better to pass over the King; the Cardinal might resent precedence conceded to the King.[39]

Wolsey assured Henry that Pope Clement would grant the annulment, and Wolsey himself wrote to Rome about the king's "great matter." He explained that Henry was very concerned that he had been living for eighteen years with Catherine, to whom he was not and could not be legally married. The king feared that their inability to have a healthy son was a punishment to him for living with Catherine, quoting a biblical passage, Leviticus 20:21, that said, "If a man shall take his brother's wife, it is an unclean thing . . . they shall be childless." "As this matrimony is contrary to God's law," Wolsey wrote to Pope Clement, "the King's conscience is grievously offended."[40]

Much to Henry's irritation, Pope Clement refused the petition. In the first place, he did not want to say that an earlier pope had been wrong. In addition, Queen Catherine had made it clear that she considered herself legally married, and Clement agreed with her. Probably he was also suspicious of Henry's motives; after all, Henry's conscience had failed to trouble him until he wanted to marry Anne Boleyn. This skeptical point of view was common, as Shakespeare slyly demonstrates in *Henry VIII*:

DUKE OF SUFFOLK: How is the king employed?

LORD CHAMBERLAIN: I left him private, full of sad thoughts and troubles.

DUKE OF NORFOLK: What's the cause?

LORD CHAMBERLAIN: It seems the marriage with his brother's wife has crept too near his conscience.

DUKE OF NORFOLK: No, his conscience has crept too near another lady.[41]

Pope Clement preferred to rely on another passage from the Bible, Deuteronomy 25:5: "If brethren dwell together, and one of them die, and have no child . . . her [the widow's] husband's brother shall . . . take her to wife." From this it could be concluded that actually Henry had been *required* to marry his brother's widow.

Perhaps the greatest complication, however, had nothing to do with contradictory Bible verses: the Holy Roman Emperor, Charles V, was Catherine's nephew. Charles was very definitely on his relative's side in this matter, and he was also just about to invade Rome. Clement, hoping to appease the emperor, refused Henry's request. Charles not only invaded Rome but took the pope prisoner.

Clement VII refused to annul Henry's marriage, leading to England's break with the Catholic Church.

Chancellor Thomas More

By 1529 Henry had grown weary of waiting for Wolsey to fix things for him, so he fired Wolsey and appointed a new lord chancellor who was neither a bishop nor even a priest. Sir Thomas More, the first layman to serve as lord chancellor, was a lawyer, judge, and writer. According to Desiderius Erasmus, one of the best-known writers and scholars of the time, More was a faithful husband, a loving and idolized father, and a persuasive orator: "In short, what did Nature ever create milder, sweeter, and happier than the genius of Thomas More?"[42] More had known the king since Henry was a child, and had served in Par-

Sir Thomas More replaced Wolsey as lord chancellor of England. A zealous anti-Lutheran, More recognized the church as the final authority in state affairs.

liament under Henry VII. Years later, More and Henry VIII had become friends, and the future lord chancellor came to know and admire Catherine as well.

In 1521 More may have helped Henry write a pamphlet called *The Assertion of the Seven Sacraments Against Martin Luther*, in which the king defended the Catholic Church's position on the sacraments and the pope against the German monk's challenges. The pamphlet proclaimed:

> What a great limb of the Devil he [Luther] is, endeavoring to tear the Christian members of Christ from their head! . . . [No punishment would be too great for one who] will not obey the Chief Priest and Supreme Judge on earth . . . [for] the whole Church is subject not only to Christ, but . . . to Christ's only vicar, the pope of Rome.[43]

Because of these and other statements in the pamphlet, Pope Leo X, the pope who had excommunicated Luther, granted Henry the title *Defensor Fidei*—Defender of the Faith. Henry was so pleased with the honor that he placed the phrase on his coins, and English monarchs claim the title to this day.

Whether or not More actually wrote any of the pamphlet, he was a zealous anti-Lutheran who certainly agreed with its content in word and in spirit. Henry was well aware of his friend's views. According to a letter that More wrote some years later, however, Henry knew also that More disapproved of the annulment plans, but he hoped that More would consider all the facts carefully and help him if he could. More wrote:

> His grace moved me again to look and consider his great matter, and . . . to

Thomas More Discusses the Pope

In this scene from Robert Bolt's play A Man for All Seasons, *the duke of Norfolk is trying to understand why Thomas More has resigned his position as lord chancellor of England.*

NORFOLK: Well, Thomas, why? Make me understand—because I'll tell you now, from where I stand, this looks like cowardice!

MORE: All right, I will—this isn't "Reformation," this is war against the Church! . . . Our King, Norfolk, has declared war on the Pope—because the Pope will not declare that our Queen is not his wife.

NORFOLK: And is she?

MORE: I'll answer that question for one person only, the King. Aye, and that in private, too.

NORFOLK: Man, you're cautious.

MORE: Yes, cautious. I'm not one of your hawks.

NORFOLK: All right—we're at war with the Pope! The Pope's a Prince, isn't he?

MORE: He is.

NORFOLK: And a bad one?

MORE: Bad enough. But the theory is that he's also the Vicar of God, the descendant of St. Peter, our only link with Christ.

NORFOLK: A tenuous [shaky] link.

MORE: Oh, tenuous indeed.

NORFOLK: Does this make sense? You'll forfeit all you've got—which includes the respect of your country—for a theory?

MORE: (*Hotly*) The Apostolic Succession of the Pope is—(*Stops, interested*) . . . Why, it's a theory, yes; you can't see it, you can't touch it; it's a theory. But what matters to me is not whether it's true or not but that I believe it to be true, or rather, not that I *believe* it, but that *I* believe it. . . . I trust I make myself obscure?

NORFOLK: Perfectly.

ponder such things as I should find therein. . . . And if . . . [there were] such things as should persuade me to the part, he would gladly have me among . . . his councillors in the matter. . . . And nevertheless he graciously declared unto me that . . . I should perceive mine own conscience . . . and that I should first look to God, and after God, unto him.[44]

It seems clear that Henry was sure that More would agree with him eventually, and equally clear that More thought Henry would not pressure him to agree. Both were wrong.

The Divine Right of Kings

Henry was thoroughly convinced that no one, not even the pope, should be able to tell him what he could or could not do. He believed strongly that he held the throne by virtue of "divine right." That is, Henry believed that because of his royal birth, his authority to rule came directly from God. Therefore his decisions were not subject to review by any man, even one generally acknowledged as God's chief representative on earth. Henry had been willing to submit to the traditional authority of the pope as long as it suited him, but now it seemed that was no longer going to be possible. Henry declared:

> Even if his holiness [the pope] should do his worst by excommunicating me and so forth, I shall not mind it, for I care not a fig for all his excommunications. Let him follow his own at Rome, I will do here what I think best.[45]

In November 1529 Henry convened a session of Parliament. He persuaded this Parliament to support his plans to produce a male heir, and, for the most part, to agree with his growing conviction that the pope had too much power over matters in England. There was not much ob-

jection on the latter score, for the English people tended to be very loyal to their king and resentful of outside interference. Henry's quarrel with the pope helped to persuade Parliament to pass several bills that reduced the authority of the church in England.

In 1530 Henry issued a notice that his government intended to prosecute a group of bishops and other clergy on rather artificial charges. The churchmen were accused of having once attempted to please Henry by taking a stand the king now chose to interpret as contrary to a fourteenth-century English law. Most of those charged were supporters of Catherine against Henry's plans. By the time Parliament reconvened in January 1531, however, Henry had decided to include in the prosecution all the clergy of England.

A Compromise

The king was willing to offer a compromise: If the priests and bishops would admit their "guilt" and offer him a "gift" of £100,000, he would drop the charges. This was a great deal of money, about as much as England's typical yearly income. They agreed to raise the money from their parishes. Henry, continuing the offensive, next demanded that the clergy acknowledge him as "the only supreme lord, and even supreme head, of the Church in England."[46] In other words, they must pledge allegiance to Henry, not to the pope, in matters of religion as well as in civil affairs. The clergy offered a number of alternative phrases, but Henry insisted on his wording. They eventually accepted it, after an important meeting

King Henry Speaks to His Nobles About the Divorce

In 1528 Henry VIII gave his own version of his request for an annulment from Queen Catherine. He made a speech to his nobles and councillors on November 8, 1528, which was recorded by Edward Hall, in his Chronicle, *and put into modern English by Hans Hillerbrand in* The Reformation: A Narrative History.

"And although it has pleased Almighty God to send us a fair daughter [Princess Mary] of a noble woman [Catherine] . . . yet it has been told us . . . that neither she is our lawful daughter nor her mother our lawful wife. . . . Think you, my Lords, that these words touch not my body and soul, think you that these doings do not daily and hourly trouble my conscience and vex my spirits. Yes, we doubt not but and if it were your own cause every man would seek remedy when the peril of your soul and the loss of your inheritance is openly laid to you. For this only cause I protest before God and . . . I have asked counsel of the greatest clerks [scholars] in Christendom . . . as a man indifferent only to know the truth and settle my conscience and for none other cause as God can judge. And as touching the Queen, if it be adjudged by the law of God that she is my lawful wife, there was never a thing more pleasant nor more acceptable to me in my life. . . . For I assure you all, that beside her noble parentage (as you all know) she is a woman of most gentleness, of most humility . . . yea, and of all good qualities appertaining to nobility, she is without comparison, as I this twenty years almost have had the true experiment, so that if I were to marry again, if the marriage might be good, I would surely choose her above all other women."

called a convocation, with the added clause, "in so far as is lawful according to the law of Christ."

The statement by the convocation was the first step away from domination by Rome, but other steps followed quickly over the next few years. In May 1532 the clergy agreed not to make any new canon law, or regulations governing the church, without the king's permission. They also

agreed that all canon law could be revised by a commission appointed by the king and that the commission could abolish any laws it felt would "not . . . stand with God's laws and the laws of your [Henry's] realm."[47] This agreement, known as the Submission of the Clergy, stated:

We your most humble subjects . . . having our special trust and confidence in your most excellent wisdom, your princely goodness . . . and also in your learning, far exceeding, in our judgement, the learning of all other kings and princes that we have read of . . .

First, do offer and promise, here unto your highness, submitting ourselves most humbly to the same, that we will never from henceforth enact . . . any new canons or constitutions provincial, or any other new ordinance . . . unless your highness by your royal assent shall license us to assemble our Convocation . . . and thereto give your royal assent and authority.[48]

In short, as historian Philip Hughes says, this document "placed the whole life of the church at the mercy of the king."[49]

The next day Lord Chancellor Thomas More resigned his position. He had failed to change either Henry's mind or his own on the matters of the king's marriage and of the pope's authority in England.

In January 1533 Henry took the public step that made his intention to break with Rome completely clear. His annulment petition was still pending, but he would wait no longer for official permission to leave Catherine and marry Anne. At this point he had not lived with Catherine for two years or more. More importantly, Anne was pregnant; a quick wedding was necessary to ensure that the hoped-for heir would be legitimate.

Henry and Anne were married secretly on January 25, 1533. Since it was clear that no annulment was forthcoming from the pope, Henry placed the issue before the convocation of bishops in England. As they were now required to make decisions based upon what was good for England

and for its king, they naturally approved his appeal. Archbishop of Canterbury Thomas Cranmer, the highest ranking English bishop, made it official by declaring the marriage of Henry and Catherine to be null and void. A few days later, in a private hearing, he pronounced that Anne was Henry's official wife. In June 1533 Anne was crowned queen of England.

Of course Pope Clement could not ignore such outright denial of his authority. In July he excommunicated King Henry, declared that the marriage of Henry and Anne was not valid, and further stated that any children they bore would be illegitimate. In September the couple's only child, the future Queen Elizabeth I, was born.

The Act of Succession

In 1534 Parliament met and passed five acts that further separated the English church from the church under the authority of Rome. The first act stated that it was no longer considered heresy to deny the authority of the pope. The second stated that all bishops in England would be appointed by the king, not by the pope. The third, a more formal version of the Submission of the Clergy, made it unlawful to enforce any part of church law that the king disapproved of, or to appeal to the courts of the pope. The fourth act forbade anyone from applying to the pope for any dispensations or special permissions; henceforth those must come from the archbishop of Canterbury. The fifth act was the First Act of Succession, stating that Henry's marriage to Catherine had been invalid and making Anne's children heirs to the throne. Every adult in England, male and female, was required to sign an oath affirming agreement with the terms of this act.

Most people obediently signed, although some did not. People of no particular importance avoided signing simply by failing to appear when signatures were being taken. They would not be missed. Those who were well known or who had powerful positions in England were objects of public and royal scrutiny, however. If they did not sign promptly, they were suspected of disloyalty to the king.

John Fisher, bishop of Rochester, had been one of Henry's most outspoken opponents since 1527, when the annulment issue first came up. He wrote, he argued, he preached, and he made it very clear that he thought Henry was wrong. He said again and again that the marriage to Catherine was legal and valid and that

Henry could never be considered the head of the church in England, since that was the position of the pope.

Sir Thomas More, the former lord chancellor, tried to remain silent about the annulment. However, he had never wavered in his belief that the king could not deny the authority of the pope. When he was called to sign the oath, he refused. He was willing to swear to support the succession; that is, to say that Anne's children would be the future monarchs of England. He was not willing to agree to the rest of the First Act of Succession, which declared the invalidity of the marriage of Catherine and Henry.

For their refusal to sign, More and Fisher were charged with treason and imprisoned in the Tower of London. By this time Henry was allowing no one to contradict his will, and he had yet to make one more major statement on the subject.

Henry VIII with his new wife and queen of England, Anne Boleyn. The couple was married on January 25, 1533, an act that signaled Henry's clear break with the church.

First Act of Succession

The First Act of Succession of 1534 stated that Catherine was no longer to be considered the queen of England, but only the widow of Prince Arthur. It also stated that Anne was queen and that any children of Anne and Henry would inherit the crown of England. This excerpt is from Hans Hillerbrand's The Reformation: A Narrative History Related by Contemporary Observers and Participants.

"The marriage heretofore solemnized between your highness [Henry VIII] and the Lady Catherine, being before lawful wife to Prince Arthur, your elder brother . . . shall be, by authority of this present Parliament, definitively, clearly and absolutely declared . . . to be against the laws of Almighty God . . . [and]utterly void and annulled. . . .

The said Lady Catherine shall be from henceforth called only dowager [widow] to Prince Arthur, and not queen of this realm . . . the lawful matrimony . . . solemnized between your Highness and your most dear and entirely beloved wife Queen Anne, shall be established, and taken for undoubtful true, sincere and perfect ever hereafter, according to the just judgment of . . . Thomas [Cranmer], Archbishop of Canterbury. . . .

Also be it enacted by authority aforesaid [i.e., Parliament] that all the issue [children] had and procreated, or hereafter to be had and procreated, between your Highness and your said most dear and entirely beloved wife Queen Anne, shall be your lawful children . . . and inherit, according to the course of inheritance and laws of this realm."

The Act of Supremacy

While More and Fisher were in the Tower awaiting judgment, Henry placed before Parliament one more act to seal his position of absolute authority. This was the Act of Supremacy of 1534, which stated quite simply that the king "is and ought to be the supreme head of the Church of England."[50] Unlike the statement signed by the convocation in 1531, the supremacy act had no provision for differences of opinion about the law of Christ; it simply meant what it said. The 1534 act also required an oath, primarily from the clergy but also from prominent men of England. Now the break with Rome was final, and the stage was set for the executions of Thomas More and Bishop Fisher. These two men of conscience were beheaded a few days apart, in June 1535.

During the twelve years that remained of Henry's life, he enacted several more policies to mark the path of the Church of England. He issued the Six Articles of

Faith, which made it clear that, unlike Luther, his break with Rome was based on organization and not doctrine. Even today, the Church of England has more similarities to the Roman Catholic Church than to other Christian denominations. Some reforms did occur under Henry, however, who encouraged the printing of the Bible in English and insisted on its availability in every church in the country.

Another consequence of the break with Rome itself was the dissolution, or breaking up, of the monasteries of England. Monasteries and other religious houses still occupied a great deal of land in England, and most of the monks and nuns who lived in them had remained loyal to Rome. Henry decided to get rid of these pockets of dissension and gain some money for the royal treasury at the same time. He declared that the monasteries were to be "dissolved" and the land returned to the crown.

Daughter of Henry VIII and Anne Boleyn, Queen Elizabeth (pictured) was predisposed to Protestantism.

Henry's Offspring

Eventually Henry fathered a son, but Anne Boleyn was not the mother. Henry's second queen was convicted of adultery and treason in 1536. For these crimes, Anne was beheaded, and less than two weeks later, the king married Jane Seymour. Their only child was to become King Edward VI. Jane Seymour died soon after Edward's birth. Henry married three more times, but there were no more children. All three of his offspring, however, followed him in ruling England. His son, Edward, took the throne at the age of nine and died six years later. His daughter Mary, whose mother was Catherine, ruled for five years before she also died. Anne's daughter, Elizabeth, became queen in 1558 and reigned until 1603, one of the most successful and popular monarchs in English history. Henry did accomplish the continuation of his own bloodline and "the quiet [of his] kingdom," although not in the way he had planned.

The separation of the Church of England from the Roman Catholic Church came about primarily because of Henry VIII's personal desire to be rid of his first wife and his political desire not to be subject to the pope's authority. But he could never have achieved what he did if there

The Dissolution of the Monasteries

This letter, written in the late sixteenth century, is from Hans Hillerbrand's The Reformation: A Narrative History Related by Contemporary Observers and Participants. *After the abbot (head of the abbey, or monastery) and all the other monks were turned out, local people often looted and vandalized the buildings.*

"They [the English officials] called the abbot and other officers of the house, and demanded all their keys, and took an inventory of all their goods both inside and outside; all the animals, horses, sheep, and cattle in pasture or grange places, the visitors caused to be brought into their presence, and when they had done so, turned the abbot with all his convent and household forth of the doors. . . .

Such persons as afterward brought their corn or hay, or such like, found all the doors either open, the locks and shackles plucked away, or the door itself taken away, went in and took what they found—filched it away. . . . It would have pitied any heart to see what tearing up of lead there was and plucking up of boards and throwing down of the spars; when the lead was torn off and cast down into the church and the tombs in the church all broken (for in most abbeys were divers [several] noble men and women—yea, and in some abbeys, kings, whose tombs were regarded no more than the tombs of all other inferior persons; for to what end should they stand when the church over them was not spared for their cause!), and all things of Christ either spoiled, carped away, or defaced to the uttermost."

had not already been discontent in England regarding the clergy and the church. Henry certainly used that discontent to get Parliament and the people of England to go along with his plans. At the same time, Parliament and the people may have been enthusiastic in their support of Henry because his plans also fit into their desires to limit the wealth and power of the clergy.

4 Reformers Become Protestants

The people of England were willing to go along with King Henry's separation from the church of Rome because they gained more local authority. In the German lands peasants and princes alike saw the new religious reformation as a way to increase their own power.

Peasant Revolts

During the late 1400s and early 1500s, peasant uprisings in the German lands were frequent occurrences. The peasants wanted justice, their own land, and freedom from control by the private armies of the local barons. By 1524 the changes in the church offered the peasants new ways to attack the existing social structure. The peasants assumed that if the power of the church was decreasing, perhaps so too was the power of the state. What is more, Luther's translation of the New Testament into German had made it available to many more people. Some began to discover in it ideas that supported their own: that Jesus always had kind sympathy for the poor and the oppressed, for example, and that the early Christians had lived together, sharing all their goods with one another.

Luther believed that the peasants misinterpreted the Bible. He was sympathetic to their plight, but he believed even more strongly in the rights and powers of the state. He told the leaders of the revolts, looking to him for support, that they were wrong in believing that the Bible viewed all men equal: "For a worldly kingdom cannot stand unless there is in it an inequality of persons, so that some are free, some imprisoned, some lords, some subjects."[51] He then encouraged the princes to suppress the revolts, as indeed they were already doing.

Peasants and their leaders felt that Luther had betrayed them, and many turned to other newly emerging religious denominations. Many German princes, on the other hand, approved of Luther's statements about the power of local rulers and gave him more and more support.

Protestants

By 1529 Germany was divided between the rulers who supported the Holy Roman Emperor and the Catholic Church and those who supported the Reformation. In that year the emperor called for a diet at the German city of Speyer to attempt to settle the matter. The assembly passed a decree that permitted Lutheran church services in the states whose princes were Lutheran, but that also required that Catholic services be allowed. At the same time, it completely outlawed Lutheran services in the Catholic states, which held the majority of the population. Six Lutheran princes and fourteen free imperial cities replied in so-called Protest that they could not in good conscience accept the decree. From this Protest came the term that soon was applied to anyone who rebelled against the Catholic Church: Protestant.

Emperor Charles V ignored the Protest, but he never seriously enforced the edict. He was too busy fighting the French to worry much about the Protestants, and he hoped and expected that a

Occupied with fighting the French, Holy Roman Emperor Charles V ignored the Protestant movement, enabling reform to continue.

council of bishops would eventually straighten out this whole religious tumult. Meanwhile, the Protestant regions continued their reforms.

The Schmalkaldic League

By 1531 the Protestant princes and cities had formed their own network, "determined to resist the emperor and the Catholic imperialists."[52] This network, called the Schmalkaldic League because the delegates first met in the city of Schmalkalden, became a powerful political force. Its origins were supposedly religious, but as historian Owen Chadwick writes, "It was not always clear whether the league was defending Protestants against Catholics or the rights of princes against the rights of the emperor; nor whether the emperor was defending Catholicism or imperial supremacy."[53] In any case, the increasing political support gave Protestant churches some peace and freedom to become established. As Christianity had come out of the catacombs and into everyday life when Emperor Constantine converted in the fourth century, so Lutheranism and other forms of Protestantism began to take hold when the political leaders accepted the new religions.

Originally Lutherans were drawn together by aspects of the Catholic Church they disliked: the power of the pope over them, monks and nuns, the financial system that awarded church offices for money, and so on. But eventually it was necessary to define themselves not only by what they rejected but by what they believed in. Protestant theology began to take shape.

Augsburg Confession

In 1530, in preparation for yet another imperial diet, this time at Augsburg, Germany, the Lutheran princes put their case in writing. The statement, written by Philipp Melanchthon, a brilliant young scholar, and presented in the names of the Lutheran princes, is called the Augsburg Confession. Melanchthon was one of Luther's most gifted followers. He came to Luther in Wittenberg and for the remaining years of Luther's life was his greatest supporter and friend.

The Augsburg Confession is the systematic statement of Lutheran belief. Much of the Confession is written so as to be as noncontroversial as possible. For example, in stating "that no one ought to teach publicly in churches or to administer the sacraments, unless duly called," it evaded the question of whether holy orders (the rite of ordination of the priesthood) was a sacrament. Catholics believed it was; Protestants did not. As another example, the Confession states "that private absolution is to be retained in the churches although it is not necessary to enumerate all sins in confession."[54] The reason given for this relaxed requirement is a practical one: Melanchthon observes that reciting all one's sins is impossible and cites a verse from the Psalms, "Who can understand his errors?"[55] Again, this was stated so generally that one could interpret

At the diet of 1530, Protestant leaders present the Augsburg Confession, the official statement of Lutheran belief.

The Augsburg Confession

The Augsburg Confession (1530) was written by Philipp Melanchthon as a statement of the Lutheran position to be presented at a diet called by Emperor Charles V. These statements from the document are excerpted from the translation that appears in Documents of the Christian Church, *edited by Henry Bettenson.*

"IV. Of Justification

They teach that men cannot be justified in the sight of God by their own strength, merits or works, but that they are justified freely on account of Christ through faith, when they believe that they are received into grace and that their sins are remitted on account of Christ. . . .

X.   Of Confession

They teach that private absolution is to be retained in the churches although it is not necessary to enumerate all sins in confession, because it is impossible, as the psalmist says, 'Who understands his offences?'

XV. Of the rites of the church

They teach that those rites are to be preserved which can be preserved without sin and which are of service for tranquillity and good order in the Church, as fixed holy days, feast-days and such like.

But men are warned not to burden their consciences in such matters, as if such observance were necessary to salvation.

XX. Of faith and good works

Our people are falsely accused of forbidding good works. . . . Our works cannot reconcile us to God or merit remission of sins and grace and justification. This we obtain only by faith, when we believe that we are received into grace on account of Christ. . . . Moreover our people teach that it is necessary to do good works, not in order to trust to merit grace thereby, but because of the will of God. . . . Hence it is readily seen that this doctrine is not to be accused of preventing good works, but much rather to be praised because it shows how we can do good works."

it in different ways. Catholics could believe that it retained the sacrament of confession. Protestants could believe that confession was permitted but not required.

The emperor read the Confession and turned it over to a commission of theologians for analysis. Their report admitted to problems in the Catholic Church. The emperor promised to help correct the problems to the best of his ability. He also stated his hope that Protestants would return to the church. They did not.

Reformed Church of Switzerland

Meanwhile, in other parts of Europe reformation was proceeding along different lines. The two strongest movements came out of Switzerland, which was then, as it is now, one of the most independent areas of Europe. The Swiss cities were and are governed locally and bound together loosely in a confederation with three official languages: German, French, and Italian. The confederation comprises twenty-two administrative divisions called cantons, which are something like counties.

Switzerland's political and intellectual independence made it the natural birthplace of a new religious movement. As one historian says, "Because of their intense loyalty to their local governments and the Confederation [the central government], the Swiss were disinclined to accept the domination of the papacy in religious matters."[56] And indeed, Renaissance humanism had taken hold very solidly in Switzerland, offering a home to Erasmus and other humanist scholars. Scholars at Swiss universities studied the Bible, looked for its original sources, and tried to improve existing translations.

The first great Swiss reformer was Ulrich Zwingli, who was only a few weeks younger than Martin Luther. He was aware of Luther's activities in the early 1520s, by which time he had already begun quietly preaching his own version of Reformation theology. Zwingli lived in the German-speaking city of Zurich. As a parish priest he preached his own explanations of the Bible and criticized practices such as indulgences and the sale of clerical positions. He also preached against private confession, monasticism, fasting, and the presence of art and music in church. All these practices, he stated, were not in the Gospels and therefore should not be part of Christian worship.

Zwingli and Luther, as well as many Protestants who came later, believed that the practice of Christianity should be based solely on Scripture—that is, on faith in what is written in the Bible. The Catholic Church had long believed that Christianity is based upon both Scripture and traditional practice—that is, not only on the Bible but also on the growing and living faith of Christians through the ages. Therefore, if pictures and music helped people to worship, then they were acceptable. If fasting helped people to examine their consciences and reject sin, then it was useful. (Later in the Reformation the English theologian Richard Hooker likened the Anglican Church—the Church of England—to a stool with three legs: Scripture, tradition, and reason.)

Zwingli, however, was convinced that he was right and that Catholic tradition was wrong. In 1522, during the season of Lent, normally a time of fasting in preparation for Easter, Zwingli preached against fasting and the practice of not eating meat. Several prominent citizens of Zurich publicly broke the fast as an expression of protest. The local bishop was appalled, but the Zurich city council decided to settle the issue at a formal disputation. Zwingli prepared his statement of beliefs, called the Sixty-seven Conclusions.

In the Sixty-seven Conclusions, or theses, he made clear his position: The whole truth of Christianity is contained in the Gospels. Zwingli believed that Jesus did not require fasting, nor that priests be unmarried. Zwingli took the position that what Jesus did not forbid is right and acceptable. The hierarchy of the church is not based upon the Bible, he claimed, but the power of the state is. Therefore, Christians ought to reject the power of the bishops and the pope, but obey their secular leaders—kings, princes, councils.

The Zurich council found Zwingli's conclusions agreeable, and ordered the priests of Zurich to "preach only what they could establish by Scripture."[57] The council also gave Zwingli the right to initiate

Swiss reformer Ulrich Zwingli was an outspoken critic of the Catholic Church. While many of his views were closely akin to Luther's, the two differed on several points, leading to the first major split in Protestantism.

any reforms in worship that he found necessary. Over the next few years, many priests married and began using the local language in services; these years also saw the introduction of simplified forms of public worship. During 1524 enthusiastic Zwinglians began to reform even the physical characteristics of the churches. As historian Harold J. Grimm relates:

> Pictures, statues, crucifixes, candles, and other ornaments were removed from the churches and destroyed, decorated walls were whitewashed, the bones of the local saints were buried, altars were replaced by tables, organs were dismantled, and the singing by choirs was abolished. . . . Little remained but bare, cold edifices which would hardly detract the attention of the worshippers from the hearing of the simple, unadorned Word of God.[58]

In keeping with their support of Zwingli's ideas of reform, the Zurich council took over the monasteries and nunneries and either closed them or turned them into schools or hospitals.

Zwingli was encouraged by these results to spread his reforms to all of Switzerland. Until his death in 1531 Zwingli worked to convince the rest of Switzerland to join his reform movement, and he saw his ideas spread to Germany, where they came in conflict with Luther's. Zwingli's version of Protestantism came to be called the Reformed Church.

The Anabaptists

Another form of Protestantism began in Switzerland and spread quickly through

Zwingli on Luther

Although Zwingli and Luther were both reformers, they did not always get along. Zwingli especially disliked being lumped with Luther in everyone's mind. In this letter to a friend, given in Hillerbrand's The Reformation: A Narrative History, *he expresses his unhappiness.*

"The high and mighty of this world have begun to persecute and hate Christ's teaching under the presence of the name of Luther. They call all of Christ's teaching 'Lutheran', no matter who on earth proclaims it. Even if one never read about Luther and is faithful solely to the Word of God, he would yet be scolded to be a 'Lutheran'. This is now my fate.

Who called me to proclaim the Gospel and to interpret an entire Gospel? Was it Luther? Why, I began to preach in this fashion long before I ever heard of Luther. For this reason I began some ten years ago to study Greek in order to learn Christ's teaching in the original language. . . . At any rate, Luther did not teach me anything. . . . The papists none the less burden me and others maliciously with such names and say, 'You must be a Lutheran, for you preach the way Luther writes.'"

Germany and into Holland and Belgium. After the peasant uprisings of 1524–1525, groups of people began studying the Bible and creating their own versions of the faith. These people came to be called Anabaptists (*ana* = again) because they believed in adult baptism. They required members who had been baptized as infants to be rebaptized.

The most radical of the Anabaptists believed in a communistic way of life. They wanted to follow the ways of the early Christians and live with their goods and property in common. They also believed that the church was called to be apart from the world. Therefore, they believed that secular rulers (kings, princes, magistrates, and so forth) could not be religious leaders as well. In this belief they set themselves against not only the Catholic Church, but the new Protestant religions as well. The Lutherans, the Reformed Church, and the Church of England all maintained close ties with political authority. These denominations regarded the Anabaptists as outlandish, radical, heretical, and dangerous.

Calvin

In the 1530s another great theologian and reformer emerged in Switzerland, this time in the French-speaking city of Geneva. John Calvin was born in France and attended the University of Paris. Like Luther, Calvin studied law because his fa-

The Reformation resulted in the emergence of new religious groups. The Anabaptists, a Protestant sect, was formed in 1523. They were widely persecuted for their radical religious beliefs, which emphasized a return to a primitive form of Christianity.

ther wanted him to. Like Zwingli, he was fascinated by the classics and was something of a humanist. He first encountered Luther's writings sometime in 1532, and was very much impressed. By 1536 he had published a book of his own, called *The Institutes of the Christian Religion.* Reissued in new editions many times during his lifetime, the book ended up over a thousand pages long. The *Institutes* became the most important expression of Calvin's faith and theology and one of the most influential books of the Reformation period.

Calvin, like Luther, believed strongly that God was immense and unknowable and that man was small and frail. Therefore, God's revealed word—the Bible— "must be our final authority, not only in religion and morals but in history, politics, everything." [59] Calvin believed that people were so disobedient and inclined to sinful acts that they could never deserve eternal happiness in heaven. Jesus' death was a sacrifice that provided salvation—but not for all. Only a few, whom Calvin referred to as "the elect," would be saved. Calvin believed that the elect were chosen for salvation before they were born, and that there was nothing they could do to lose salvation, just as there was nothing anyone else could do to obtain it.

We say rightly that [God] foresees all things, even as he disposes of them; . . . When we attribute foreknowledge to God, we mean that all things have always been and eternally remain under his observation. . . . We call predestination the eternal decree of God by which he decided what he would do with each man. For he does not create them all in like condition, but ordains some to eternal life, the others to eternal damnation.[60]

For Calvin, the true church was composed only of the few elect: living, dead, and not yet born. He felt that the elect would naturally find themselves drawn to a life of faith, and that the visible church on

Calvin's City Ordinances

John Calvin essentially governed Geneva and made ordinances and laws about all aspects of life. These are some of his ordinances, from Hillerbrand's The Reformation: A Narrative History.

"The whole household shall attend the sermons on Sunday, except those left at home to tend the children or cattle.

If there is preaching on weekdays, all who can must come. . . . Those who have men-servants or maid-servants shall bring them whenever possible, so that they shall not live like animals without instruction. . . . Anyone coming after the sermon has begun is to be warned. If he does not amend, he is to pay a fine of three sous. . . .

Those who are found to have rosaries or idols to adore are to be sent before the Consistory. . . . The same applies for those who go on a pilgrimage. Those who observe feasts or papal fasts shall only be admonished. Those who go to mass shall, besides being admonished, be sent before the council, which will consider the punishment of the offenders by imprisonment or special fines, as it judges best.

No one shall invite another to drink under penalty of three sous.

Taverns shall be closed during the sermon, under penalty that the tavern-keeper shall pay three sous, and whoever may be found therein shall pay the same amount.

Anyone singing indecent, licentious songs, or dancing . . . shall be kept in prison three days and then sent to the council."

French theologian John Calvin was converted to Reformation doctrines after encountering Luther's writings in 1532. After Luther's death, Calvin's views continued to shape the Reformation in France, Bohemia, Poland, parts of Germany, Holland, and Scotland.

Calvinism took firm hold in Geneva, and the canton became a theocracy—a government ruled by a religious authority. Calvin himself ran Geneva for twenty years. He set up rules of conduct and insisted that they be followed strictly. Playing cards, dice, and dancing were outlawed. Everyone attended five sermons a week. Clothing, dress, and hairstyle were regulated. Everyone had to obey the rules; there were no exemptions on the basis of social position. Ministers and elders visited homes to check on their congregations.

Why did people go along with this rather grim way of life? Because Calvin presented to them a way to live close to God. They could place high ideals over materialistic pleasures. Those who were able to follow the rules without stumbling could feel fairly confident that they were among the elect.

Calvinism spread to France, Bohemia, Poland, southern Germany, Holland, and Scotland, taking hold primarily among townspeople. Everywhere adherents relied on Calvin's books and writings, especially the *Institutes*, but reading and reflecting on the Bible formed the core of their worship service. They followed the Genevan model of organization, with ministers, elders, and deacons composing church hierarchy. Eventually, Calvinists came to be called Presbyterians, because their churches were run by elders, or presbyters.

earth would then be composed of "all those who, by a confession of faith, an exemplary life, and participation in the sacraments of baptism and the Lord's Supper profess the same God and Christ with ourselves."[61] Unlike the Anabaptists, Calvin believed that church and state were designed to work together, with the state enforcing rules of morality dictated by the church.

5 Changing Europe: Society During the Reformation

When Luther and Zwingli were still schoolboys and Calvin not yet born, Christopher Columbus sailed across the unknown Atlantic. He found not Japan and China, as he had expected, but the part of the world that would later be known as North and South America. In 1519, while Luther was writing in defense of his Ninety-five Theses and before he had been excommunicated, Ferdinand Magellan and Sebastian del Cano set sail on a voyage around the world. Magellan died before the voyage was completed, but del Cano returned to Europe with one ship out of the original five, landing three years after the voyage began.

Maps drawn in 1517, at what we consider the beginning of the Reformation,

Christopher Columbus (left) and Ferdinand Magellan (right) helped pave the way for the Reformation by broadening people's worldviews.

would have shown the West Indies and bits of the South American coastline, but not the two great continents of North and South America. Only ten years later, Diego Ribero was able to draw maps of the world "which show the coasts of Europe, Africa, and Southern Asia with great accuracy, the east coast of the Americas from New-foundland to the Straits of Magellan, and the west coast from Peru to Mexico."[62]

These explorations were not only of interest to scholars; they had an impact on everyday life as well. New food plants—tomatoes, potatoes, chiles, chocolate, maize (corn), strawberries—came from the Americas to Europe and Asia, changing European and Asian cuisine forever. What we think of as inherent characteristics of regional cooking—potatoes in Irish food, tomatoes in Italian food, even chiles in Szechuan Chinese food—all came to those regions as recently as the sixteenth and seventeenth centuries. As food historian Raymond Sokolov says, before 1492, "From one end of Europe to the other people ate much the same food. . . . The French, Italian, and Spanish food 'traditions' we now think of as primeval all sprang up relatively recently and would be unrecognizable without the American foods sent across the water, mostly in Spanish boats."[63]

The people who welcomed new foods and looked for new adventures in the New World shared the outlook of those who welcomed new ways of looking at God and the church, and explored new ways to worship. The world seemed to be expanding every day. If a person's relationship to the world was different from what he or she had always thought, might not the individual's relationship to God and the church also be different?

The discovery of previously unknown lands also made Europeans aware that Christianity, rather than being a world-wide religion, was mainly European. There were different ways of believing in Asia, in Africa, and in the Americas—and there were vast continents potentially available for conversion to Christianity as well. Luther mentioned the New World twice in his writings, declaring that preachers would spread the gospel westward, where it might find a welcome home. And the Catholic Church gained more new converts in the Americas than it lost to Protestantism in Europe.

The Printing Press

Just in time for the Reformation, a revolution in printing occurred in Germany. Probably around 1454, Johan Gutenberg, a citizen of Mainz, experimented with movable metal type and produced what is usually considered the first type-printed book, a Bible. In 1470 a Frenchman named Guillaume Fichet wrote a letter in great excitement about the wonderful invention: "There has been discovered in Germany a wonderful new method for the production of books, and those who have mastered the art are taking it from Mainz out into the world. . . . The light of this discovery will spread from Germany to all parts of the earth."[64]

Certainly it seemed as if all the world had been waiting for the arrival of printed books so that it could begin to read them. One scholar wrote to a friend:

> At this very moment, a whole wagon load of classics . . . has arrived from

Johan Gutenberg invented movable metal type in the middle of the fifteenth century. This new invention provided reading material to the public, spurring the diffusion of both Catholic and Protestant views.

Venice. Do you want any? If you do, tell me at once, and send the money, for no sooner is such a freight landed than thirty buyers rise up for each volume, merely asking the price, and tearing one another's eyes out to get hold of them.[65]

Printed books made it possible for anyone to own a Bible, and thus to follow Luther's suggestion to follow the Gospels and become one's own priest. In fact, Luther himself referred to the printing press as "God's highest and ultimate gift of grace by which He would have His Gospel carried forward."[66] Certainly it advanced the spread of Luther's ideas. Because of the printing press, the Ninety-five Theses were spread throughout Germany in a matter of weeks, and many of his later works became immediate best-sellers. Correspondingly, the works of his opponents also spread rapidly by way of printed copies. In 1524 Erasmus remarked jokingly that "in Germany hardly anything is salable except Lutheran and anti-Lutheran writings."[67]

The printing press enabled enthusiasts on all sides to spread their views widely. There was, as one historian describes it, "a torrent of pamphlets, cartoons, and caricatures which carried to the masses the basic tenets of the Reformation, outcries against social and political grievances, polemical thrusts and broadsides, and radical revolutionary programs."[68] In 1518 there were about 150 book titles printed in Germany. In 1524 there were nearly a thousand, 80 percent of which favored Luther's Reformation.

Cities and Banking

The influx of gold and silver from the Americas and the increase in trade all over the world helped the development of another major trend: banking. From an

The Power of the Press

In this excerpt from a 1554 letter quoted in The Reformation: A Narrative History, *Ignatius of Loyola, founder of the Society of Jesus, discusses the ways in which the press can be used to fight Protestantism.*

"The heretics [Protestants] write a large number of booklets and pamphlets, by means of which they aim at taking away all authority from the Catholics, and especially from the society [of Jesus]. . . . It would seem expedient, therefore, that ours [that is, the society] here also write answers in pamphlet form, short and well written, so that they can be produced without delay and bought by many. In this way, the harm that is being done by the pamphlets of the heretics can be remedied and sound teaching spread. These works should be modest, but lively; they should point out the evil that is abroad and uncover the . . . deceits of the adversaries."

economy that was largely agricultural and that operated primarily by barter, Europe became a capitalist economy: that is, using capital (money) to make more money. Spices and silks imported from Asia could not be completely paid for by exports, so gold and silver were used to fill in the gaps.

As the volume of transactions increased, so did new ways of dealing with money: Bills of exchange, letters of credit, and drafts (checks) all came about as ways of transferring large sums of money without having to move around physical quantities of gold or silver. All of these types of exchanges were done by bankers, a new breed of businessmen. The most powerful bankers of the Reformation period belonged to the Fugger family, who made their own fortune by loaning money to Emperor Charles V.

Charles V had borrowed heavily from the Fugger bank in order to pay off the electors who voted for him. Jacob Fugger was so confident of his own position of power and wealth that he sent a letter to the emperor demanding repayment of the loan:

> It is well known that your Majesty without me might not have acquired the Imperial honor [the crown], as I can attest with the written statements of all the delegates [the electors of Germany]. . . . And in all this I have looked not to my own profit. . . . My respectful request is that you will graciously . . . order that the money which I have paid out, together with the interest on it, shall be returned without further delay.[69]

The concept of using money as payment and the idea of lending money at interest extended to other areas of society. Where once a peasant would have performed some service for a lord or paid tribute in agricultural produce, now he would owe a payment of money. Where once farming was the means to provide food for families, now it was also a way of making a product that could be sold at a profit. Where once laborers were hired to perform the work necessary to support a manor or a business, now laborers were seen as yet another ingredient in the process of creating new wealth.

In the mid–fourteenth century the epidemic of bubonic plague called the Black Death had drastically reduced Europe's population, but the number of people began to grow rapidly during the fifteenth century. Bad weather in the early sixteenth century limited food supplies. More people and less food made prices rise, and people were increasingly unwilling to reduce their own share of food by giving a tenth to their landlord and another tenth to the church, in accordance with the custom of the times. As one historian says, "They were increasingly reluctant to share their diminished wealth with lazy monks and ignorant clergy, with silk-clad cardinals and the papacy at Rome."[70] Luther played to this feeling when he wrote his *Address to the Christian Nobility of the German Nation*:

> How is it that we Germans must put up with such robbery and extortion of our goods at the hands of the pope? . . . Why do we Germans let them make such fools and apes of us? . . . And we still go on wondering why princes and nobles, cities and endowments, land and people grow poor. We ought to marvel that we have anything left to eat![71]

Meanwhile, more and more people were living in towns instead of on farms. Many were the bankers, merchants, and craftspeople who conducted their business in towns and took advantage of the increased use of money as a means of exchange. Some were laborers who helped to manufacture the new goods available for sale. These townspeople tended to be ambitious, looking for ways to make themselves as wealthy and powerful as nobles. They liked the Reformation emphasis on individual initiative rather than the older model, which had looked to the church and the state as the central authority with responsibility for everyone.

Of course, although all of Europe faced the same economic conditions, not all of Europe became Protestant. Nevertheless it is fair to say that the difficulties of the common people made them more open to the ideals of the Reformation.

Art

Throughout the Middle Ages and the Renaissance, art, literature, and education had been sponsored almost exclusively by the church. The universities had been founded to train priests. Most significant art had been created to decorate churches. Great architectural advances had been made to create cathedrals for the greater glory of God.

The Reformation temporarily caused a decrease in art production. Zwingli's Reformed Church actively discouraged the use of art and music in connection with religion—nothing was to distract from the preaching of the word of God. Luther and Calvin were willing to accept beautiful church art because nothing in the Bible specifically forbade it, but Zwingli and other radical reformers adhered to an ex-

Many Reformation leaders discouraged the creation or use of church art—or anything that would distract from the word of God. (Left) Lutheran artists like Albrecht Dürer, however, created beautiful woodcuts and paintings. (Right) In Catholic Italy, Renaissance artist Michelangelo continued to produce art for the church.

tremely rigid interpretation of the second commandment, which forbids the possession of "graven images."

Much art was created as part of the propaganda war. Lucas Cranach illustrated Luther's pamphlets and books, for example. Albrecht Dürer, another Lutheran, made beautiful woodcuts and paintings that expressed Lutheran interests in Bible-related subjects. Hundreds of broadsheets and pamphlets were produced with illustrations that supported Catholics or Protestants. Meanwhile, in Catholic Italy,

great Renaissance artists like Michelangelo continued to produce their work for the glory of God and the church.

Music

Music in the Reformation changed as well. During the Middle Ages church music was primarily sung by a male choir, in Latin, as part of the Mass. The Protestants began to incorporate songs in their own language

Luther the Musician

Martin Luther was a fine musician as well as a scholar and a theologian. He wrote hundreds of hymns. His most famous effort, "Ein Feste Burg," expresses his concept of a God who is mighty and powerful and majestic beyond all human understanding. This nineteenth-century translation by Frederick H. Hedge appears in the Methodist Hymnal.

Ein Feste Burg (A Mighty Fortress)

A mighty fortress is our God, A bulwark never failing;
Our helper He, amid the flood of mortal ills prevailing.
For still our ancient foe doth seek to work his woe;
His craft and power are great, and armed with cruel hate—
On earth is not his equal.

Did we in our own strength confide, our striving would
    be losing;
Were not the right man on our side, the man of God's
    own choosing.
Doth ask who that may be? Christ Jesus, it is He!
Lord Sabath [of hosts] is His name, from age to age
    the same;
And He must win the battle.

And tho' this world, with devils filled, should threaten to
    undo us;
We will not fear, for God hath will'd, his truth to
    triumph though us.
The Prince of Darkness grim—We tremble not for him;
His rage we can endure, For lo, his doom is sure,
One little word shall fell him.

That word above all earthly powers, No thanks to them
    abideth;
The Spirit and the gifts are ours, Through Him who with
    us sideth;
Let goods and kindred go, this mortal life also;
The body they may kill; God's truth abideth still,
His kingdom is forever.

into their church services. Luther himself loved music and wrote many hymns, including the famous "Ein Feste Burg," known in English as "A Mighty Fortress Is Our God." In 1524 Luther and some friends produced the first Protestant hymnal, including melodies and words from sources as varied as Catholic hymns and folk songs. Luther declared, "The devil has no right to all the good tunes."[72]

Zwingli, in keeping with his belief in simplicity, did not allow music in church. Calvin permitted singing if the whole congregation sang in unison. Catholic composers such as Palestrina continued to produce intricate vocal and instrumental works for the Mass.

Schools

Until the Reformation, schools were almost exclusively training grounds for priests. Luther, who saw immediately that it would be necessary for reformers to establish their own schools to replace the

While a spirit of scientific inquiry took shape during the Reformation, Nicolaus Copernicus's heliocentric theory was generally unwelcome among Catholics and Protestants.

church-run institutions, was very disappointed that Lutheran princes and lords did not rush to do this. In 1524 he complained, "In the German provinces, the schools are now everywhere allowed to go to ruin."[73] Luther dignified the profession of teaching by regarding it as a vocation, or calling.

Luther's great follower and assistant, Philipp Melanchthon, spent much of his life attempting to revive old schools and begin new ones. The various religious groups each eventually found it necessary to start their own schools and universities, since most were limited to students who followed the beliefs of the school's founder. Protestants were not allowed to attend Catholic universities, Calvinists were excluded from Lutheran schools, and so on. Eventually many schools came under civil, or secular, control.

Science

The era of the Reformation was also a time of scientific revolution. When Nicolaus Copernicus first stated that the earth moves around the sun, his heliocentric theory, as it is called, did not gain much attention. His great work (*De revolutionibus orbium coelestium—On the Revolution of the Celestial Orbs*) was published in 1543, but its main elements were known in learned circles as early as 1530. In 1539 Luther discussed the Copernican theory at his home. The discussion was recorded by one of his followers:

> There was mention of a certain new astrologer who wanted to prove that the earth moves and not the sky, the sun, and the moon. This would be as if

Copernicus on Planetary Motion

Copernicus's first statement about the motion of the planets around the sun was written about 1514, but only a few copies circulated, mainly among the astronomer's friends. This modern translation is excerpted from Will Durant's The Reformation.

"1. There is no one center of all the celestial circles or spheres.

2. The center of the earth is not the center of the universe. . . .

3. All the spheres [planets] revolve about the sun as their mid-point, and therefore the sun is the center of the universe. . . .

5. Whatever motion appears in the firmament [sky] arises not from any motion of the firmament, but from the earth's motion. . . .

6. What appears to us as motions of the sun arise not from its motion but from the motion of the earth and our sphere, with which we revolve around the sun like any other planet. . . .

7. The apparent retrograde and direct motion of the planets arises not from their motion but from the earth's. The motion of the earth alone, therefore, suffices to explain so many apparent inequalities in the heavens."

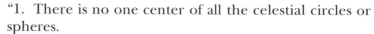

Copernicus's heliocentric theory, which stated that the earth moves around the sun.

somebody were riding on a cart or in a ship and imagined that he was standing still while the earth and the trees were moving. [Luther remarked,] "So it goes now. Whoever wants to be clever must agree with nothing that others esteem. . . . This is what that fellow does who wishes to turn the whole of astronomy upside down. . . . I believe the Holy Scriptures, for Joshua commanded the sun to stand still, and not the earth."[74]

Melanchthon took the theory much more seriously, but he also quoted the Bible against Copernicus. The Catholic Church made no objection to the theory as long as it was merely a suggested possibility. When people began treating it as established fact, the church balked, as the Italian astronomer Galileo Galilei was to find out. He was excommunicated and imprisoned in 1633 for refusing to state that Copernican theory might not be true.

Neither Catholics nor Protestants welcomed this new theory, which turned their understanding of the universe upside down. In their defense it must be noted that heliocentrism went against thousands of years of scientific inquiry and the conclusions of an awesome array of astronomers. Moreover, Copernicus's initial calculations for the orbits of the planets were very complicated. Not until Galileo, Johannes Kepler, and Isaac Newton worked out the mathematics in better detail and greater simplicity did heliocentrism become generally accepted.

The Role of Women

In the sixteenth century a woman's place was related more to her social class than to any other factor. European women played the traditional roles of mothers, housekeepers, and helpers to their husbands. City women were more likely to know how to read than their country sisters. There were well-educated women of the upper classes, but not many. A woman who knew Latin was said to be "learned beyond her sex."[75] As the century progressed, the availability of printed books, especially Bibles in French, German, and English, allowed more women the possibility of studying on their own.

The major reformers were ambivalent on the subject of women. Luther—who had married a former nun—spoke fondly and proudly of his wife and her intelligence. On the other hand, he also said:

> Men have broad shoulders and narrow hips, and accordingly they possess intelligence. Women have narrow shoulders and broad hips. Women ought to stay at home; the way they were created indicates this, for they have broad hips and a wide fundament [bottom] to sit upon, keep house and bear and raise children.[76]

In discussing the duties of ministers in the church, Luther said, "The Holy Spirit has excepted women, children, and incompetent people from this function, but chooses . . . only competent males to fill this office."[77]

Despite this sort of reaction, many women took prominent roles in the Reformation. Marguerite d'Angoulême, sister of King Francis I of France, was a Protestant. Her writings influenced many, and she provided a welcoming haven for Protestant reformers. She and her daughter, Jeanne d'Albret, queen of Navarre, supported Calvin at the beginning of his career, when he most needed such prominent and wealthy followers.

In the latter half of the sixteenth century the Reformation would turn violent. Both Catholic and Protestant women would be martyred for their causes, but women took advantage of their role to act on their faith in more subtle ways as well.

A Protestant Woman's Role

In this excerpt from an essay on French city women of the Reformation, historian Natalie Z. Davis offers a look at the ways in which ordinary Protestant women could participate. The essay is found in Davis's Society and Culture in Early Modern France.

"And what could a city woman accomplish for the cause if she were not rich and powerful like a noblewoman? On a Catholic feast day, she could defy her Catholic neighbors by sitting ostentatiously spinning in her window. She could puzzle over the Bible alone or with her husband or with Protestant friends. If she were a printer's wife or widow, she could help get out a Protestant edition to spread the word about tyrannical priests. She could use her house for an illegal Protestant conventicle or assembly. She could put aside her dissolute [sluttish] hoop skirts and full gowns and start to wear black. She could harangue priests in the streets. She could march singing songs in defiance of royal edicts. She could smash statues, break baptismal fonts, and destroy holy images. She could, if persecution became very serious, flee to London or Geneva, perhaps the longest trip she had ever taken. She could stay in France and dig the foundations for a Reformed temple. She could even fight—as in Toulouse, where a Huguenot woman bore arms in the First Religious War. And she could die in flames, shouting to her husband, as did one young wife of Langres, 'My friend, if we have been joined in marriage in body, think that this is only like a promise of marriage, for our Lord . . . will marry us the day of our martyrdom.' "

A Protestant woman, for example, could choose a Catholic feast day to "defy her Catholic neighbors by sitting ostentatiously spinning in her window."[78] A Catholic woman could hide a hunted priest in her home or provide a private place for the celebration of Mass.

The Reformation affected individual women's lives by involving them in actions of passive or covert resistance, but it did not profoundly affect the position of women in society as a whole. The Protestants did not overthrow the social order. Women continued to fulfill their traditional roles. Not until the twentieth century did women become involved in significant numbers in the ministry of Protestant churches, and not until very recently have women been ordained to the priesthood in the Church of England.

6 Religious Wars and Persecution

Roman Catholic, Lutheran, Calvinist, Reformed, Anabaptist, Anglican (Church of England)—these were the major Christian denominations in Europe in the mid-sixteenth century. Each held different interpretations of the Bible, different beliefs about the sacraments, and different practices, and each was convinced that its beliefs were the right ones. Increasingly, philosophical differences intensified disputes over property or privilege, and before long the war of words erupted into persecution and war in earnest.

Zwingli Versus Luther

Martin Luther and Ulrich Zwingli were born only a few weeks apart and began their own versions of reformation at almost the same time. Yet each resented the idea that he owed anything to the other. Zwingli wrote irately to a friend, "They call all of Christ's teaching 'Lutheran' no matter who on earth proclaims it. . . . Luther did not teach me anything."[79] In a similar spirit, Luther wrote to staunch supporter and fellow reformer Johannes Brenz:

> I wonder what kind of a man Zwingli is, since he is so ignorant of grammar

and dialectic [logical presentation of arguments], to say nothing of the other arts, yet ventures to boast of victories. That kind of glory quickly leads to embarrassment.[80]

Luther and Zwingli's most heated argument centered on the meaning of the sacrament of communion. Luther retained the Catholic belief that Jesus was actually present in the bread and wine of communion, derived from the statement of Jesus at the Last Supper, "This is my body." For Luther, the Bible meant what it said. If Jesus said, "This is my body," then the bread he had blessed and distributed to his disciples was his body. Zwingli, on the other hand, believed that the word *is* should be interpreted to mean "signifies." He believed that the bread and wine represented the body and blood of Jesus but were not literally these substances.

Both Luther and Zwingli believed that everyone should read the Bible, but neither would tolerate interpretations of the Bible different from his own. Said Luther: "In a word, either they or we must be ministers of Satan. There is no room here for negotiation or mediation."[81] For both men, as well as for many others seeking the absolute during this turbulent period, being right was the most important thing in the world—much more important than being merciful.

The result of these disagreements was that each group set up its own institutions. Not only churches but also schools and often entire towns were segregated. Lutherans were not permitted to enroll in universities set up by members of Zwingli's Reformed sect, and vice versa. Certain towns or villages became strongholds of one group or another, and nonbelievers were driven out.

Switzerland in Turmoil

After Zwingli's successes in Zurich, Switzerland became divided into Catholic and Reformed cantons. Zwingli was so determined to prevail that he set up a blockade to keep staples such as salt from reaching Catholic areas, making the already beleaguered Catholic cantons even more desperate. In 1531 they assembled an army and sent it against Zurich in the battle of Kappel. Zwingli himself fought with the Zurichers and died on the battlefield. After the engagement the victorious Catholic army had Zwingli's body quartered and burned, as suited a heretic.

England After Henry VIII

Henry VIII died in 1547, having established the Church of England with himself as its first head. Although officially Henry's revolt was against the authority of the pope, his ultimate goal—besides satisfying his personal desires—was the peace and unity of England. By the time of his death, Protestant ideas from Germany and Switzerland had crossed the channel and taken hold among a number of prominent citizens, but another fifty years would pass before England could be said to have

The death of Zwingli at Kappel, in a battle between the Catholic and Reformed cantons of Switzerland.

King Edward VI of England, a sickly child who ruled from 1547 to 1553. Under his reign, Thomas Cranmer introduced the Book of Common Prayer.

achieved the religious stability Henry sought.

The next king of England, Edward VI, was nine years old when he succeeded his father to the throne. Because of Edward's youth, one of his mother's brothers was named lord protector and helped him to rule. This uncle, Edward Seymour, the duke of Somerset, favored Protestantism and used his position to advance its cause. Young Edward had been raised as a Protestant and welcomed his uncle's suggestions regarding religion. During Edward's brief reign, Parliament passed a law requiring the removal of all pictures of prophets, apostles, and saints. According to historian Will Durant:

Most of the stained glass in the churches was destroyed; most of the statues were crushed; crucifixes were replaced with the royal arms; white-washed walls and stainless windows took the color out of the religion of England. There was a general scramble in each locality for church silver and gold; and in 1551 the government appropriated what remained. The magnificent medieval cathedrals barely remained.[82]

Thomas Cranmer, archbishop of Canterbury, was inclined to the ideas of Martin Luther. In 1549 he produced the first English-language prayer book for the Church of England. The *Book of Common Prayer* was designed to retain as much Catholic doctrine as possible, as well as familiar forms of worship consistent with desired reforms. Both Cranmer and Somerset aimed to advance their Protestant ideas while keeping the peace and avoiding controversy.

Bloody Mary

Edward VI died in 1553 and his half-sister Mary, the daughter of Henry VIII and Catherine of Aragon, took the throne. Mary had been raised a Catholic, mostly in Spain, and considered herself more Spanish than English. She certainly had no particular reason to love the English, who had failed to support her mother during the years in which Henry had attempted to divorce her.

As queen, Mary at first attempted to be conciliatory. She was a devout Roman Catholic, but she knew that much of England was not. Thus she was in the awkward position of being the legal head of a denomination not her own, namely, the Church of England. An uneasy truce reigned between Mary and her subjects.

Then Mary announced her plans to marry King Philip II of Spain, the son of her father's longtime adversary Charles V. Rebellion erupted. The British could live with a Catholic queen, but many feared the combination of Catholic and Spanish domination. Some prominent citizens began to plot against Mary.

Mary responded by repealing laws legitimizing the Protestant religion and cracking down on Protestants. From 1555 to 1558 a total of 273 Protestants were burned at the stake in England. Of these, 51 were women and 5 were bishops, including Archbishop Cranmer. Many more Protestants fled to the European continent

Mary tried to stem the Protestant tide in England. While her efforts were futile, her methods were ruthless. Under Mary, many Protestants were burnt as heretics, earning her the name Bloody Mary.

Protestant Martyrs

In this selection, quoted in The Protestant Reformation *by Lewis Spitz, Florimond de Raemond of Bordeaux, France, marvels at the martyrs of the Reformation.*

"Meanwhile, fires were being kindled everywhere. . . . The stubborn resolution of those who were carried off to the gallows, where they were seen, for the most part, to be deprived of life rather than courage, stupefied several people. Because when they saw innocent, weak women submit to torture so as to bear witness to their faith, facing death calling out only to Christ, the Savior, and chanting various psalms . . . men exulting upon seeing the dreadful and frightful preparations for and implements of death which were readied for them, and half charred and roasted, they looked down from the stakes with invincible courage. . . . They were like rocks standing against waves of sorrow, in short they died while smiling."

Burned at the Stake

In his 1563 publication, The Book of Martyrs, *about the English Protestants burned at the stake during the reign of Bloody Mary, John Foxe included this story.*

"Shortly after the death of Thomas Cranmer [in 1556], three men were burned together in one fire at Salisbury: John Maundrel, husbandman [farmer]; William Cobberly, tailor; and John Spicer, freemason. . . .

They were examined before the sheriff . . . and some popish [Catholic] priests of the parish. . . . Asked how they believed, they replied that they believed as Christian men ought to believe, in the Father, Son, and Holy Ghost; in the twelve articles of the creed; and in the Holy Scripture from the beginning of Genesis to the Apocalypse [Revelation]. This did not satisfy the chancellor; did they, he asked, believe that the words of consecration changed the sacrament of the altar to leave no bread and wine, but only Christ's body and blood? They told him that they did not, adding that the popish Mass was abominable idolatry and injurious to the blood of Christ. . . .

Asked if they believed the pope to be the supreme head of the church and Christ's vicar on earth, they said that Christ was the head of his church, and under Christ, the queen's majesty. 'What,' said the chancellor, 'a woman head of the church?' 'Yea,' they answered, 'within her grace's dominions.' . . . Regarding the images in the church, John Maundrel said that wooden images were good to roast a shoulder of mutton, but evil in the churches, leading to idolatry. . . .

Brought to the stake on 23 March 1556, . . . they declined the queen's pardon vehemently. 'Not for all Salisbury,' said John Maundrel, and John Spicer remarked, 'This is the joyfullest day that ever I saw.' Two stakes were set, and to these they were bound; one fire sufficed.

Cobberly burned longer than the other two; his flesh was scorched and his left arm was burned to the white bone, but still he stood. Then he stooped over the chain and knocked with his stiffened right hand upon his breast; blood and matter ran out of his mouth, and he hung there. Suddenly, when everyone thought him dead, his body again rose upright."

to escape the persecution for which the queen came to be known as Bloody Mary.

Protestantism Restored

Mary died in 1558 and her half-sister Elizabeth became queen. Elizabeth, the daughter of Anne Boleyn, had been raised Protestant. Like Mary, she had been declared illegitimate and had spent much of her youth in the shadows of the court. She was even imprisoned in the Tower of London for a brief time during Mary's reign. Many people had hoped that a Roman Catholic would succeed Mary, and they had a candidate in mind: another Mary, the daughter of James V of Scotland and Mary of Lorraine. This young woman, who is known to history as Mary, Queen of Scots, had the support of two Catholic countries, France and Spain. More people in England favored the daughter of Henry VIII, however, and were willing to give Elizabeth a chance.

By 1559 Parliament had "restore[d] the supremacy of the Church of England to the crown of the realm," and England was once more Protestant.[83] The church issued thirty-nine Articles of Religion in 1563, precisely defining Anglican beliefs. In the same year, clergyman John Foxe published his *Book of Martyrs*. Far from being an objective statement of faith, this blatant piece of propaganda denounced the papacy and lionized the Protestants who had been martyred under Mary's regime.

Many Roman Catholics remained loyal to their denomination, and now it was their turn to face persecution, if not outright prosecution. In most cases private worship, although illegal, was tolerated, but subtle forms of persecution persisted. For example, Catholics could not hold certain offices. The very fact that they had to attend Mass in secret indicated their second-class citizenship. Wealthy Catholic families built private chapels in their homes, usually including "priest's holes"—secret cupboards where they could hide not only altar cloths and communion vessels but a priest as well, should the government decide to make a raid. Some Catholics did refuse to recognize the queen's authority and were executed for treason. By the end of Elizabeth's reign in 1603, Protestantism was firmly established in England.

Religious Wars in France

The course of the Reformation in France is a prime example of the rise of politics' determining matters of religion rather than religion's directing affairs of state. The kings of France remained loyal to Rome during the first half of the sixteenth century, when the French were much more concerned with fighting among themselves and against their traditional enemies, Spain and the Holy Roman Empire. Although both King Francis I of France and Emperor Charles V were Catholic, they spent most of their time battling each other and ignoring the growth of Protestantism in their countries.

By midcentury there were a large number of Protestants in France, many of them nobles like Marguerite d'Angoulême, the Calvinist sister of King Francis. French Calvinists, called Huguenots, had grown sufficiently in numbers and importance during the first half of the century to establish the first formal and open French Calvinist church in Paris in 1555.

Henry II, who succeeded his father, Francis I, in 1547, continued the wars against Charles V and his successor, Philip II of Spain. The next year Henry II, who was more alarmed by Protestant advances in France than Francis had been, established the *chambre ardent*, or court of fire, to try religious heretics. Thousands of people were accused of heresy, and the numbers increased every year.

The strongest Catholic faction in France was the Guise family. They wanted to gain control of the monarchy and stamp out Protestantism in France, and they were prepared to call in help from Germany or Spain, if necessary, and to "set aside the succession and make themselves the masters of France in order to prevent a Protestant from coming to the throne."[84] The Huguenots in their turn were prepared to seek help from England, Sweden, and the Schmalkaldic League in order to knock the Catholics off the throne.

Then Henry II died and was succeeded by his young brother, Charles IX. Henry's widow, Catherine de Médicis, the queen regent, was responsible for governing while her brother-in-law was a minor. Wanting to avoid war with Spain or England and hoping to persuade the French to settle their own affairs, she called a meeting of the different religious parties. Calvin sent one of his ablest followers, Theodore Beza, to state the Protestant side. Beza, however, not only refused to reconcile with the Catholics, he also offended the Lutherans by insisting on the Calvinist explanation of communion.

Catherine did not give up her attempt to create peace and in 1562 convinced the government to issue the so-called Edict of January. This official proclamation allowed Huguenots to worship publicly outside of town walls and to worship privately within towns. This was more than the Guises could stand.

> When the Duke of Guise with an armed escort came upon some Huguenots worshiping in a barn, he ordered them to leave and they answered with cries of "papist and idolator." Stones flew. The duke's armed retainers fired and killed 63 out of six or seven hundred worshipers. This set off the wars.[85]

The Huguenots responded by demolishing Catholic churches and destroying statues, pictures, and consecrated communion bread. This sort of fighting went on for ten years, with both sides behaving badly. One bishop said of these years:

> If I say to a Catholic, "Of what religion were you six months ago?" he answers, "I was of the Catholic religion." Then I say to him, "Do you call that religion Catholic which permits the violation of public faith, the exciting of seditions, the pillaging and strangling of brothers?" And if the same question were addressed to one of the Reformed and he admitted his adherence, I would say, "What abominable [loathsome] reform has authorized you to overturn altars, profane sacred vessels, and commit the most revolting excesses against persons consecrated to God? Both of you should give up names which do not befit you, because the Christian religion has nothing in common with the profession of brigands."[86]

"What Could a Woman Do?"

King Henry IV of France describes his mother-in-law, Catherine de Médicis. Catherine provoked the St. Bartholomew's Day Massacre, but Henry thinks that all in all she performed a delicate balancing act. The king's analysis is found in the Durants' The Age of Reason Begins.

"I ask you, what could a woman do, left by the death of her husband with five little children on her arms, and two families in France who were thinking of grasping the crown—ours [the Bourbons] and the Guises? Was she not compelled to play strange parts to deceive first one and then the other, in order to guard, as she did, her sons, who successively reigned through the wise conduct of that shrewd woman? I am surprised that she never did worse."

Catherine de Médicis, queen regent for Charles IX, was a key planner of the St. Bartholomew's Day Massacre.

St. Bartholomew's Day Massacre

Catherine de Médicis, still attempting to reconcile the two groups, proposed a marriage between her daughter Margaret (a Catholic) and Henry of Navarre. Henry was the son of Jeanne d'Albret and grandson of Marguerite d'Angoulême and had been raised as a Huguenot. All the Guises and their Huguenot enemies were invited to Paris for the wedding, which took place on August 18, 1572.

Much political plotting went on during the week of wedding festivities, during which Duke Henry of Guise convinced Catherine that the Huguenots would not be satisfied until all France was Protestant and a Protestant was on the throne. Apparently Catherine panicked and decided it was time to get rid of all of the Huguenot leaders. She convinced the young king, her brother-in-law, that the Huguenots were planning to murder them both.

Early in the morning of August 24, 1572—St. Bartholomew's Day—conspirators under orders of King Charles IX attacked Huguenot leaders in Paris and elsewhere in France. Mobs joined in the violence and thousands of Huguenots were murdered. To make matters even worse, the royal court celebrated the massacre by holding a mass of thanksgiving. The reaction of Pope Gregory XIII was equally inappropriate: He gave a sermon praising God for the success of the murderers and ordered a medal struck to commemorate the event.

Pro-Catholics slaughter thousands of French Huguenots on St. Bartholomew's Day, August 24, 1572.

"Paris is worth a Mass"

The Huguenots became more determined than ever to resist Catholic persecution and wars continued on and off for another fifteen years. In 1574 Charles IX died without an heir; the next king of France, Charles's brother Henry III, died in 1589, also leaving no children. The throne went next to Henry of Navarre (Henry IV), whose marriage had preceded the St. Bartholomew's Day Massacre.

Henry waffled between the Calvinism under which he was raised and Roman Catholicism, depending on the political situation. When he became king the Catholics of Paris refused to allow him to take the throne, even though he pledged not to persecute them. So Henry spent ten years besieging Paris in an attempt to assume the throne. The combination of Catholic resistance from within the city's walls and Spanish help successfully kept him from entering the city, and eventually he realized that he was never going to succeed by force. The southern parts of France had large Huguenot areas, but by far the majority of the French population remained Catholic. So Henry took the practical way out: He converted to Catholicism. Henry, for whom religion had never been of utmost importance, reportedly announced the decision with the lighthearted words, "Paris is worth a Mass."[87]

Henry's goal was peace. In 1598 he issued the Edict of Nantes, which guaranteed religious freedom in France. Huguenots were granted the right to live anywhere in France, "free from inquisition, molestation or compulsion to do anything in the way of Religion, against their conscience." The edict prohibited both

Villagers mock French Huguenots, who continued to be persecuted years after the St. Bartholomew's Day Massacre. Despite such activity, Protestantism survived as a religion.

sides from baptizing children forcibly into their faith, "under penalty of exceptionally severe punishment." More importantly, Huguenots were permitted to hold "any office or position in this Realm." Also, "no distinction [was] to be made . . . in the reception of pupils for education in universities, colleges and schools, nor in the reception of the sick and needy into hospitals, almshouses or public charities."[88] The very need for such statements indicates the kind of discrimination and persecution that existed over differences in religious beliefs.

Edict of Nantes, 1598

This treaty between Henry IV of France and the Huguenots remained in effect for about eighty years, until Louis XIV overruled it. Some of its terms, as given in Bettenson's Documents of the Christian Church, *are quoted here.*

"III. We ordain that the Catholic, Apostolic and Roman faith be restored and reestablished in all those districts and places of this our Realm . . . in which its exercise has been interrupted, there to be freely and peaceably exercised. . . .

VI. And to leave no occasion for trouble or difference among our subjects: we permit those of the so-called Reformed Religion to live and abide in all the towns and districts of this our Realm . . . free from inquisition, molestation or compulsion to do anything in the way of Religion, against their conscience . . . provided that they observe the provisions of this Edict. . . .

XIII. We most expressly forbid to those of this religion the practice thereof, in respect of ministry, organization, discipline or the public instruction of children, or in any respect, in our realm and dominion, save in the places permitted and granted by this Edict.

XIV. The practice of this religion is forbidden in our court and suite, in our domains beyond the mountains, in our city of Paris, or within five leagues thereof. . . .

XXI. Books concerning this religion are not to be printed and exposed for sale save in towns and districts where the public practice of the said religion is allowed.

XXII. No distinction is to be made with regard to this religion, in the reception of pupils for education in universities, colleges and schools, nor in the reception of the sick and needy into hospitals, almshouses [homeless shelters] or public charities. . . .

XXVII. Members of this religion are capable of holding any office or position in this Realm."

Why Persecution?

Why did Christians battle, persecute, torture, and kill fellow Christians? It was certainly not to defend a belief that people had the right to worship as they pleased. The Calvinist reformer Theodore Beza said that religious liberty was "a most diabolical dogma [belief] because it means that every one should be left to go to hell in his own way."[89] Each religious group was fighting for its own liberty, not that of others. Each felt strongly that its way was the right and only way. Of course, what might be considered baser motives—political considerations, consolidation of power, financial gain—often played their part.

Historian Roland Bainton identifies three components of a disposition to persecute: "A man must believe that he is right, that the point in question is important, and that coercion is effective."[90] Each religious group felt that it was right, that its particular interpretation of Scripture was that which God intended, and therefore one could not but agree.

On the second point, too, there was no question: Matters of salvation were important. It was believed that "man's eternal destiny as well as his social well-being" depended on worshiping rightly and belonging to the true church.[91] This attitude had developed over more than a thousand years of Christianity. And the church and the community were deeply interrelated. Anyone who did not believe in the church could seriously disrupt the entire community. Persecuting and even killing someone who wanted to tear down the social order could be likened to cutting off an arm to save the body from infection.

On the third point, sixteenth-century persecutors believed firmly in the value of forcing people to change their ways (if not their beliefs). One contemporary humanist said, "It is no great matter, whether they that die on account of religion be guilty or innocent, provided we terrify the people by such examples."[92] But persecution also creates martyrs, like those in John Foxe's famous tract, and hypocrites, like Henry IV of France. An Italian observer in the sixteenth century noted that one who attempts to force people to one religion or another is like the fool "who having a great barrel with a little wine in it, fills it up with water to get more. But instead of increasing the wine he spoils what he had."[93]

7 The Catholic Response: Counter-Reformation

Despite the accusations of Luther, Zwingli, and other reformers, the Catholic Church in the sixteenth century was not blind to its need for reform. Humanist scholars were already looking at ways to put the church back to rights by working from within. They wanted popes and bishops to be more spiritual and less worldly. They wanted monks to obey the rules of their orders. They wanted parish priests to be better educated and to preach good, inspiring sermons to their congregations. They did not want or expect any major changes in the doctrines of the church.

There had been many "reformations" in the church over the 1,500 years of its existence. Frequently they had come about because of great scholars or inspired and inspiring men and women. In the past, reform movements had often found expression in the establishment of new religious orders: The Order of Friars Minor (the Franciscans), the Dominicans, and others had formed in this way.

Reforming Orders

During the late fifteenth and early sixteenth centuries, a number of reformers attempted to create a better church within the bounds of the existing church. These reformers believed that reformation begins, as historian Philip Hughes says, "purely as a re-forming of self."[94] They believed in serving God by taking care of the sick and suffering, by preaching God's word to the people, and by living in a simple, loving manner.

One group of priests who embraced these beliefs was known as the Theatines, from one of their founders, Gaetano of Thiene. Formed in Italy in 1523, their goal was "to be merely the kind of priest priests should be."[95] They said Mass daily, they preached in the streets of Italian cities, they worked with poor people in hospitals and jails, and they heard confessions everywhere. They became known for their strict observance of priestly duties. Over the next hundred years, more than two hundred of their number became bishops who believed in reform.

About the same time, another group of Italians, this time women, gathered together under the direction of Angela Merici and dedicated themselves to the education of girls, especially poor girls. They named themselves Ursulines, after St. Ursula. After Angela Merici's death the Ursulines became an order of nuns and their work spread to France, where they

The Jesuit Plan

Ignatius of Loyola, the founder of the Society of Jesus, suggested some methods to stop Protestantism in this 1554 letter, found in Hillerbrand's The Reformation: A Narrative History.

"The heretics [Protestants] have made their false theology popular and presented it in a way that is within the capacity of the common people. They preach it to the people and teach it in the schools, and scatter booklets which can be bought and understood by many, and make their influence felt by means of their writings when they cannot do so by their preaching. Their success is largely due to the negligence of those who should have shown some interest; and the bad example and the ignorance of Catholics. . . . Hence it would seem that our Society [the Jesuits] should make use of the following means to put a stop and apply a remedy to the evils which have come upon the Church through these heretics.

In the first place, . . . it would be good to make a summary of theology to deal with topics that are important but not controversial. . . . There could be more detail in matters controversial, but it should be accommodated to the present needs of the people. . . . The abler students could be given higher courses which include greater detail. . . . The principal conclusion of this theology, in the form of a short catechism, could be taught to children. . . .

Another excellent means for helping the Church in this trial would be to multiply the colleges and schools of the society in many lands. . . . The better among our students could be sent to teach the Christian doctrine on Sundays and feast days. . . . Thus, besides the correct doctrine, they would be giving the example of a good life, and by removing every appearance of greed they will be able to refute the strongest argument of the heretics—a bad life, namely, and the ignorance of the Catholic clergy."

were a strong force for Catholic education and reform after the religious wars.

Yet another Italian reforming order arose in the 1520s, when a young man named Matteo da Basci led a group of friends, mostly Franciscans, in the same type of work that the Theatines were doing: preaching in the streets, caring for the sick and the poor, and observing great devotion to the Bible and the sacraments.

Ignatius of Loyola founded the Society of Jesus after undergoing a religious conversion in 1521. The Society of Jesus was the most important new religious order of the sixteenth century.

Matteo wanted to return the Franciscans to the ideals of the founder of their order, St. Francis of Assisi. He insisted upon the poorest of living conditions, and he and the others wore beards and a traditional coarse brown habit with a four-pointed hood. From this hood, which was called a *cappucio* in Italian, came the name of the order: *cappuccinos*, or Capuchins.

The Jesuits

The most important new religious order of the sixteenth century was the Society of Jesus, known popularly as the Jesuits. (The name Jesuit was originally coined as an insult by Calvin, but it caught on and members of the society have used the name ever since.) The Society of Jesus was started by a young Spanish nobleman, Ignatius of Loyola.

Ignatius was born in 1491 in northern Spain. He was raised to be a soldier and received little education as a boy. In 1521 he was wounded in battle and spent a long period of recovery in a castle. There, having read a book on the life of Jesus and another on the lives of the saints, he underwent a religious conversion and made a vow to become a different kind of soldier: a soldier for Christ.

By nature Ignatius was very much like Martin Luther. Like Luther, he worried about the salvation of his soul, but he went about dealing with the worry in a very different way. In 1523 he began to study to prepare himself for his new life. From 1528 to 1535 he studied at the University of Paris, where he began to attract a group of friends and followers. He developed a program of meditation and prayer called *The Spiritual Exercises*, a four-week program intended to help the participant put his or her spiritual life in order and become more deeply committed to following the Gospels.

While in Paris, Ignatius persuaded two friends, Francis Xavier and Peter Faber, to try the *Exercises* under his direction. They became dedicated to Ignatius and to his goal of converting others to Christianity. In 1534 the three of them and seven others created an informal organization and committed themselves to do whatever the pope needed to have done. In 1540 Pope Paul III officially established the Society of Jesus.

The Jesuits, in the words of one historian, "were an elitist corps and accepted into membership only the most intelligent, dedicated, physically strong and attractive men of sound character."[96] The Society required an extremely rigorous period of training and education. As a result, the Jesuits quickly became the most influential group in the Catholic Church. Jesuit missionaries traveled the world seeking to convert unbelievers to Christianity. They founded schools and colleges everywhere they went. Jesuits were among the first to explore the American continents, and they carried their message to India, to China, and to Japan. Europeans of the sixteenth and seventeenth centuries learned much of what they knew about Asia, Africa, and the Americas from the reports of Jesuit missionaries.

Jesuits also pursued their mission in Europe. Even in Germany, some Protestant lands were won back to the Catholic

Jesuits were described as an elite group, consisting of "only the most intelligent, dedicated, physically strong and attractive men of sound character."

Church through the work of the Jesuits. Once the Society was established, no further German provinces became Protestant.

Teresa of Ávila

Another important name in the history of Catholic mysticism in the period of the Reformation was Teresa of Ávila, who died in 1582 at the age of sixty-seven and who was canonized in 1622. Teresa, a Carmelite nun, had a powerful mystical experience, which she described in a book called *Vida* (*Life*), which many found inspirational. She reformed the Carmelite sisters in Spain and demanded a return to the values that Jesus preached in the Gospels. All Christians, said Teresa, "are called to be mystics . . . *everyday* mystics who find God within themselves and bring God joyfully to others."[97] Teresa's joyful view of life and God was in stark contrast to the grim outlook of many of the Protestants. As one historian says, "One gets the impression that if Teresa had met John Calvin she would have slapped him on the back and told him not to take himself so seriously."[98]

Councils

The traditional way to make changes in the Catholic Church was to convene a council, a gathering of bishops who discussed the issues of concern to the church at that moment in history. As an expression of the "collected wisdom of all Christendom," the pronouncements of a council held great weight.[99] In 1512 Pope

Pope Leo X replaced Julius II. During his papacy, he tended to dismiss Luther as a mere nuisance rather than a real threat to the Catholic Church. By the time Leo died in 1521, the Protestant revolt was firmly rooted.

Response to Luther

Leo X and the popes who followed him made frequent misjudgments in their dealings with Luther and the other reformers. Because the popes were rulers of a political unit, the Papal States, as well as leaders of the Catholic Church, they often found that their desires and motives conflicted. Pope Leo, for example, was much more concerned with playing a role in the election of Emperor Charles V than he was in entering into a dialogue with Luther. He considered the Ninety-five Theses and the controversy that followed to be a mere squabble among monks. He merely wrote a letter to the head of Luther's order, the Augustinians, and told him to control Luther, who was upsetting people.

When Leo died in 1521 the Protestant revolt was well under way, and it was clear that the church would have to respond in some substantive way. The cardinals elected Pope Adrian VI, who had every intention of cleaning up some of the abuses in the church. He wrote to a group of German princes and bishops:

> We are well aware that even in this Holy See [the papacy] much that is detestable has appeared for some years already—abuses in spiritual things, violation of the commandments—and that everything has been changed for the worst. . . . All of us, prelates [cardinals and other high-ranking bishops] and clergy [priests], have turned aside from the road to righteousness and for a long time now there has been not even one who did good. . . . Then, just as from here the sickness proceeded, so also from here recovery and renewal may begin.[100]

Julius II called a general council at the Lateran basilica in Rome. As this was the fifth council to occur at that place, it is known as the Fifth Lateran Council. By the time the council had completed all of its sessions in 1517, Julius had died and had been replaced by Pope Leo X. The council lasted until March of 1517, just months before Luther published his Ninety-five Theses.

The one decree that was enacted before Julius II died indicates that the church was indeed aware of some of the problems that Luther and others were concerned about. The decree stated that if it were determined that a pope had bought his election, whether with money or promises of favors, the election would be invalidated. This was a step in the right direction, but the rest of the council descended into squabbling and accomplished little of significance.

The bishops felt that such an attitude threatened their own interests, and they resisted any change that might make them less comfortable. Adrian tried to enlist the help of Erasmus. The famous scholar and humanist was too ill to come to Rome, but he advised Adrian to get rid of some of the bishops and collect a group of Catholic scholars who could have a reasonable and peaceful dialogue with the Lutherans. Adrian died after only two years as pope, and never had an opportunity to push through his reforms.

Adrian was followed by Pope Clement VII, whose reign saw several countries reject the pope's authority: not only the England of Henry VIII, but also most of Germany, Denmark, and Sweden.

In 1534 Clement was followed by Paul III, who, like Adrian, really wanted to make changes in church administration. He tried to set up several meetings with the Lutherans, but all early plans fell through. Finally, in 1541 he sent Cardinal Gasparo Contarini to a conference with the Protestants at Ratisbon (now Regensburg), in Germany. Melanchthon attended the conference as Luther's representative.

At Ratisbon the two sides actually made some attempts to reconcile. On May 3, 1541, Cardinal Contarini wrote to another bishop, "God be praised! Yesterday the Catholic and Protestant theologians came to an agreement on the doctrine of justification."[101] They agreed as well on statements about baptism, confirmation, and other areas of dispute, but a combined statement on communion was beyond them. Already, less than twenty-five years after Luther's Ninety-five Theses, the

By 1521, the Protestant movement was well under way, and members of the papacy felt its far-reaching effects. (Left) During the reign of Pope Clement VII several countries rejected the authority of the papacy. (Right) Paul III attempted to reconcile with the Lutherans and clean up church administration.

Fearing invasion by Charles V, King Francis I of France (pictured) promoted religious discord between Charles and the Protestants so that Germany would remain unstable.

Reformation was so firmly established that it was impossible for either side to compromise on so fundamental a doctrine.

Politics and Popes

Meanwhile, the political situation was making matters even murkier. Pope Paul III began to worry that if Emperor Charles V did not have the Protestants to worry about, Germany would become too peaceful and united, allowing Charles to turn his attention to Italy. For years the emperors had hoped to take over the Papal States and prevent the popes from having any political power.

King Francis I of France had similar reasons for not wanting peace in Germany. He also feared invasion. In fact, Francis was hoping to form an alliance with the Lutherans to keep Charles off guard. He offered to support the pope against Charles if Paul would refuse to reconcile with the Lutherans. Paul had religious reasons for not making peace with the Protestants, but he clearly had political reasons as well.

The next two popes (Julius III and Marcellus II) did nothing to affect matters either way. Then in 1555 the papal election went to Cardinal Giovanni Caraffa, who chose to be called Paul IV. He was seventy-nine years old, but firm and strong in his beliefs. According to the Florentine ambassador, "The Pope is a man of iron, and the very stones over which he walks emit sparks."[102] Paul IV hoped to get the Spanish and imperial troops out of Italy, and so went to war. But his legions were badly outnumbered, and his defeat signified the end of the papacy's hold over the Holy Roman Empire.

Censorship

No longer at war, Paul IV began to think in terms of mending wrongs within the church. In 1559, the last year of his papacy, he published the first Index of Prohibited Books, a list of books no Catholic was supposed to read. The list included all of Luther's works, as well as translations of the Bible the church considered heretical. Censorship of books was not new, but only occasionally was it enforced over the years. In 1559 Paul IV turned over the enforcement of censorship to an arm of the church known as the Inquisition.

The Inquisition was established in 1217 to identify and punish heretics—those whose beliefs differed from the beliefs formally accepted by the church—through a network of investigators, trials, and prisons. During the early Renaissance the Inquisition was not a major force in European society. Paul III, however, reorganized the Inquisition in 1542, under Cardinal Giovanni Caraffa, the future Paul IV.

Caraffa's rules for the Inquisition included the following:

1. When the faith is in question, there must be no delay, but on the slightest suspicion rigorous measures must be taken with all speed. . . .

4. No man must debase himself by showing toleration toward heretics of any kind, above all toward Calvinists.[103]

Paul was determined to rid Rome of heresy at all costs, sometimes fanatically so. "Even if my own father were a heretic," he is reported to have said, "I would gather the wood to burn him."[104]

The Council of Trent

In 1559 Paul died. The next pope, Pius IV, allowed the Inquisition to continue, but informed the inquisitors that they "would better please him were they to proceed with gentlemanly courtesy than with monkish harshness."[105] His major contribution to history, however, was to bring to a successful conclusion the eighteen-year-long ecclesiastical wrangling known as the Council of Trent.

Soon after the failure of the Ratisbon conference in 1541, reform-minded bishops began pushing for another general council. Pope Paul III rather reluctantly called a council to meet in Trent (now Trento, in northern Italy). By choosing an Italian city on the south side of the Alps, yet also within the Holy Roman Empire,

The Inquisition was established in the thirteenth century by the Catholic Church to combat heresy. Often, the penalty for heresy was death by burning. In 1542, Paul III reorganized the Inquisition to counter Protestantism.

Call for a Council

When Pope Paul III called for a general council to meet at Trent in 1542, he used these words, found in Hillerbrand's The Reformation: A Narrative History.

"Even though there must be, according to our faith, 'one flock and one shepherd of the flock of our Lord' [John 10:16] for the strengthening of the pure Christian community and the hope of heavenly things, the unity of Christendom has been torn apart by division, controversy and heresy. . . .

In the midst of this vehement storm of heresy, discord and war, we are called to guide responsibly the ship of Peter [the papacy]. We put little trust in our own strength, but cast all our cares on the Lord to sustain us [Psalm 55:22] and equip our hearts with firmness and our spirits with insight and wisdom.

We reflected that our truly enlightened and holy predecessors often convened, in times of great danger of Christendom, general councils and assemblies of bishops as the best and most appropriate means of salvation. Therefore we also considered the possibility of such a council."

[Here the pope discusses the times and places he had previously hoped to hold a council, all of which were unsuitable for one reason or another.]

Thus we decided that the general council is to convene on 1st November [1542] at Trent. We consider this location appropriate, since German bishops and prelates can easily [get] there, as can Spanish and French bishops, as well as others, without too much difficulty. We have decided on the date in light of the fact that the time appears sufficient to announce this decision to all Christian peoples and allows enough travel time to the prelates. . . .

Thus we decide, proclaim, summon, order and rule . . . that on 1st November 1542, in the city of Trent, which is a convenient, free, easily reached place, a general, holy council is to begin, continue, and, with God's help, to his honour and glory and the salvation of all Christendom, be concluded and perfected."

the pope not only allowed the Italian bishops easy access but also satisfied the German desire to have the council in their domain.

The council opened in 1545 with thirty bishops present. The pope did not attend. At first the members spent time trying to figure out exactly what they were supposed to do: The emperor wanted to reform abuses in the church and make some sort of peace with the Lutherans; the pope wanted to deal with questions of doctrine. Eventually the bishops decided to try to deal with both agendas at the same time.

The Council of Trent met in twenty-five sessions from 1545 to 1563, attended by hundreds of bishops. The bishops concluded that it would not do any good to try to appease the Protestants: By the 1550s there were so many different versions of Protestantism that it would be impossible to make any one denomination happy without offending several others. So the bishops decided that their contribution would be to issue the definitive statement of Catholic belief, especially in the areas that had been brought into question by the Protestants.

Trent restated the church's unwavering belief in the importance of both Scripture and tradition as the means of salvation, contrary to non-Anglican Protestants' belief in Scripture alone. The bishops refused to support any reform that diminished papal supremacy, and they ruled that the Catholic Church remained the sole authoritative interpreter of the Bible, asserting that henceforth the Latin version translated by St. Jerome in about A.D. 400, the so-called Vulgate edition, was the official version. Most of the Protestant churches had eliminated seven Old Testa-

A 1556 woodcut portrays the sacrament of baptism. Baptism, along with Eucharist (communion), was accepted as a sacrament by both Catholic and Protestant churches.

ment books and the Greek-language portions of two others from that version, declaring that these were apocryphal (not authentic).

The council reaffirmed Catholic belief in seven sacraments: baptism, confirmation, Eucharist (communion), marriage, holy orders, penance (confession), and anointing of the sick. Most of the Protestant churches accepted only two: baptism and communion.

Trent did not depart from the position of previous councils in dealing with the issue of communion. The bishops reasserted the church's belief in the actual

The Council of Trent

The Council of Trent made a number of statements of the beliefs of the Catholic Church. These are a few of them, found in Bettenson's Documents of the Christian Church.

"[The Council of] Trent . . . perceiving that this truth and this discipline [that is, the teachings of Jesus] are contained in written books and in unwritten traditions, which were received by the Apostles from the lips of Christ himself, or, by the same Apostles, at the dictation of the Holy Spirit, and were handed on and have come down to us; . . . this Synod [Council] receives and venerates, with equal pious affection and reverence, all the books both of the New and the Old Testaments, . . . together with the said Traditions."

On Eucharist:

"Since Christ our Redeemer said that which he offered under the appearance of bread was truly his body, it has therefore always been held in the Church of God, and this holy Synod now declares anew, that through consecration of the bread and wine there comes about a conversion of the whole substance of the bread into the substance of the body of Christ our Lord, and of the whole substance of the wine into the substance of his blood."

On penance:

"That penance is . . . truly and properly a sacrament in the Catholic Church, instituted for the faithful by Christ our Lord, for their reconciliation to God whenever they fall into sin after baptism."

transformation of the bread and wine into the body and blood of Christ. They also reaffirmed its corollary, belief that Jesus is sacrificed for the sins of the people each time the Mass is celebrated. (Protestants varied in their belief about the real presence of Jesus in the bread and wine, but were generally united in believing that communion was only a memorial of Jesus' sacrifice, not a reenactment of it.)

Justification, the issue that had caused Luther's soul-searching, prompted one of the lengthiest and most heated debates at Trent. Luther and the Protestants who followed him believed that faith alone was needed for salvation. The Catholic Church, taking its stand from the Book of James, had always emphasized that "faith without works is dead."[106] There was great dissent on the issue even among the bishops. The debate at Trent grew so violent, in fact, that

> one bishop clutched another by the beard and plucked out a handful of hairs; hearing which, the Emperor sent the Council word that if it could not quiet down he would have a few prelates [bishops] thrown into the Adige [River] to cool them off.[107]

With a little semantic sleight of hand the council managed to combine both beliefs: Trent ultimately agreed with Luther that God freely grants justifying grace, without any necessity for a person to do anything to "earn" it first. Trent then said that people do play a role in justification: By their own free will they must accept or reject God's grace. And the way to acceptance lay in doing good works and participating in the sacraments. This point went against not only Luther's belief but Calvin's as well: Calvin's doctrine of the elect left no room for free will to accept or reject that election.

Results of Trent

The Catholic Church emerged from the Council of Trent stronger in many ways than it had been at the beginning of the century. Though it had avoided radical reform, Trent put an end to the clerical abuses to which so many of the reformers had objected. For example, after Trent it was no longer possible for a man to hold more than one bishopric at a time. Thus was removed one avenue to corruption—the temptation to increase one's wealth and power via the taxes collected from multiple areas. One of the most significant reforms had to do with the education of priests. Trent established ground rules for the seminary system of training that persist to this day. Based on the Jesuit model of disciplined, well-run academies turning out scholar-priests, the new system ensured that priests—and the bishops who came from the ranks of the priests—would be well-educated and uniformly trained professionals.

The bishops of Trent, aiming to present a strong, united front against the Protestants, managed to reform Catholic doctrine and practice as well. Though some of the diversity that had been an important element of the church for 1,500 years was sacrificed in the name of unity, the Council of Trent succeeded in defining Catholic beliefs in a way that was both very specific and broadly authoritative. By choosing certain expressions of belief, it rejected others, even others that till then had been considered legitimate. As one historian puts it, "What came out of Trent was a Catholic 'package' which, until Vatican II [the Second Vatican Council, in the 1960s], was considered by Catholics and Protestants alike as the only possible embodiment of authentic Catholicism."[108]

8 The Reformation Spreads

By the middle of the sixteenth century Protestantism was firmly established on most of the European continent. Realizing compromise was inevitable, in February 1555 Emperor Charles V called a diet at Augsburg to make peace between the Catholic and Lutheran princes of Germany. They agreed to disagree on religious matters and set about settling the political problems arising from their religious differences.

In the agreement Charles ratified seven months later, the so-called Peace of Augsburg, each elector, prince, and free imperial city was to choose between Lutheranism and Catholicism. Those Protestants who did not accept Melanchthon's Augsburg Confession of 1530 (Calvinists, Zwinglians, and Anabaptists) were specifically excluded from the Peace. In territories ruled by a prince or other noble, all subjects were required to follow the religious preference of the ruler. A Catholic person in a Lutheran principality or a Lutheran person in a Catholic territory had only the freedom to pack up and leave. In the free cities, both Lutheran and Catholic citizens were to be allowed to worship freely.

All church lands seized by Lutherans prior to 1552 were to be retained by the Lutherans. On the other hand, any Catholic bishop, priest, or abbot who be-came Protestant after the Peace of Augsburg would forfeit his land, income, and other revenues to the Catholic Church. Finally, the Peace allowed free immigration between provinces:

> In case of our subjects, whether belonging to the old religion [Catholic] or to the Augsburg Confession, should intend leaving their homes, with their wives and children, in order to settle in another place, they shall neither be hindered in the sale of their estates after due payment of the local taxes nor injured in their honour.[109]

The Netherlands

The Netherlands held an interesting position in the mid–sixteenth century. The country was under the rule of Spain, the most powerful of the Catholic nations. At the same time, it was surrounded by Protestant influences. The strongly Lutheran northern provinces of Germany were to the east. England, both Protestant and anti-Spanish, was just across the North Sea to the west. France, to the south, was fighting religious wars and conceding rights to the Huguenots.

The Dutch, like the Swiss, were historically independent minded. They lived mainly in cities, enjoying a strong economy based on trading and banking. By the 1560s two distinct political factions existed. One was Catholic and in favor of the power of the crown. The other was composed of both Catholic and Protestant nobles who wanted to decrease the power of the Spanish rulers. The latter party advocated tolerance for the Protestants, on the practical ground that there were already too many of them to try to suppress. Historian Owen Chadwick describes the situation:

> The Catholic ruler of the Netherlands was a foreign and absent ruler, Philip II of Spain. The party which wanted toleration . . . easily appeared as the

As a prince, William III of Orange converted to Calvinism and led the Protestant movement in the Netherlands.

Philip II of Spain, the Catholic ruler of the Netherlands, declared that "he would rather die a hundred deaths than be king over heretics."

> party of patriots, the defenders against foreign armies. On the other side the party of the crown possessed an advantage. . . . The king could call upon the wealth and troops of the strongest military power of the day.[110]

Not only did Philip tax the Netherlanders heavily, he declared that "he would rather die a hundred deaths than be king over heretics."[111] As in France, tensions erupted into violence. The local prince, William of Orange, tried to remain moderate for a time, but eventually became a Calvinist and took over the leadership of the Protestant movement, which also opposed domination by Spain. Ultimately, the country became divided into a Protestant

(Calvinist) north and a Catholic south—the precursors of modern-day Holland and Belgium, respectively.

Calvinism Spreads

Despite the nearness of the Lutheran states of Germany, it was Calvinism that took hold in the Netherlands and elsewhere in Europe, largely because of the more efficient organization of the Calvinist churches. In Calvin's model, the church at Geneva, there were four levels of office: pastors, teachers, elders, and deacons, as well as a ruling body called a consistory. Each office performed an exclusive function: pastors preached and administered the sacraments; teachers gave instruction in the faith to young people, from elementary age to college; elders supervised the lives of the congregation and made sure everyone was following the rules; deacons were responsible for taking care of the sick and the poor. In Calvin's Geneva, the consistory was composed of the city's twelve elders, or presbyters, each of whom was responsible for one section of the city, and five pastors.

This system of organization resulted in a set of self-contained church organizations, each one independent of the political state in which it existed. Compared to Lutheranism, Calvinism was clear and precise and more appealing to the hardworking and literal-minded townspeople. Besides the Netherlands, Calvinism made some temporary gains in eastern Europe, especially in Poland and Hungary, but strong kings and Jesuit missionaries took those areas back to Catholicism by the end of the century.

The Thundering Scot

Calvinism's greatest success came in Scotland, and thereby to North America. Scotland experienced the Reformation late. Lutheranism, though practiced in Scotland as early as the 1520s, was repressed by King James V. The Scottish monarchy was closely connected to Catholic France, through the marriage of the king to Mary of Lorraine, whose brothers were the Guises of France. Mary of Lorraine became the regent after James's death in 1542, because their daughter, later known as Mary, Queen of Scots, was still an infant. The young Mary was raised a Catholic in France.

In 1546 George Wishart, a Protestant leader, was tried and burned for heresy by Cardinal David Beaton of Scotland. A few months later some of Wishart's friends murdered Cardinal Beaton and took over his castle at St. Andrew's, holding it for more than a year. One of Wishart's followers was a former priest and teacher named John Knox, known as the "thundering Scot."

French troops coming to the aid of the queen regent took Knox and the rest of the rebels captive. All were sent to France and forced to serve as galley slaves. Knox escaped to England in 1549, but fled to Geneva when the Catholic Mary came to the English throne in 1553. He loved the Calvinist city of Geneva, writing in 1556 that it "is the nearest perfyt [perfect] school of Chryst that ever was in the erth since the dayis [days] of the Apostillis [apostles]."[112]

From Geneva he wrote (in 1558) *The First Blast of the Trumpet Against the Monstrous Regiment of Women*, a diatribe aimed

"The Thundering Scot"

Sir Peter Young describes John Knox to the Calvinist minister Theodore Beza in this excerpt from a letter dated 13 November 1579, found in Hillerbrand's The Reformation: A Narrative History.

"In bodily stature he was rather below the normal height. His limbs were straight and well proportioned; his shoulders broad; his fingers somewhat long. His head was of medium size, with black hair; his appearance swarthy, yet not unpleasant. His countenance, which was grave and stern, though not harsh, bore a natural dignity and air of authority; in anger his very frown became imperious. Under a rather narrow forehead his eyebrows rose in a dense ridge; his cheeks were ruddy and somewhat full, so that it seemed as though his eyes receded into hollows. The eyes themselves were dark-blue, keen and animated. His face was somewhat long, with a long nose, a full mouth, and large lips of which the upper one was slightly the thicker. His beard was black, flecked with grey, thick, and falling down a hand and a half long."

Reformation leader John Knox ardently preached Protestantism in Scotland.

at the "three Marys": Mary of Lorraine; her daughter, Mary, Queen of Scots; and Henry VIII's daughter Mary, queen of England. Wrote Knox:

To promote a woman to bear rule, superiority, dominion, or empire above any realm, nation, or city is repugnant to nature, contumely [contemptuous]

John Knox's Articles

In John Knox's History of the Reformation in Scotland *(1586), he states some of the articles of belief of his Kirk [Church] of Scotland. This version is given by Harry Emerson Fosdick in his* Great Voices of the Reformation: An Anthology.

"1. First, that images are not to be had, nor yet to be worshipped.

2. That relics of saints are not to be worshipped. . . .

7. That after the consecration in the Mass, there remains bread; and that there is not the natural body of Christ. . . .

10. That every faithful man or woman is a priest. . . .

15. That the pope and the bishops deceive the people by their pardons.

16. That Indulgences ought not to be granted to fight [in the Crusades]. . . .

21. That in no case is it lawful to swear.

22. That priests might have wives, according to the constitution of the law. . . .

32. That the pope is the head of the kirk [church] of Antichrist.

33. That the pope and his ministers are murderers.

34. That they which are called principals in the Church, are thieves and robbers."

to God, a thing most contrarious to his revealed will and approved ordinance, and, finally, it is the subversion of good order, or all equity and justice.[113]

In 1559 Knox returned to Scotland at the request of the Scottish Protestants. In 1557 a group of Protestant leaders in Parliament, calling themselves the Lords of the Congregation of Jesus Christ, had signed the first Scottish Covenant, calling for a "reformation in religion and government," and demanding that the queen regent allow them to "use ourselves in matter of religion and conscience as we must answer to God."[114] Now the Lords of the Congregation promised Knox protection if he would come back to Edinburgh and preach the Reformation there.

Upon his return Knox preached a sermon against idolatry (the worship of objects as gods) and against the Catholic Mass that sparked violence. When a priest attempted to celebrate Mass, a young man who had heard Knox called out that it was idolatry. According to Knox, the priest then

gave the child a great blow, who in anger took up a stone, and casting at the priest, did hit the tabernacle [the container for the consecrated commu-

John Knox, known popularly as the "thundering Scot," preaches a powerful sermon to his followers.

nion bread] and broke down an image; and immediately the whole multitude that were about cast stones, and put hands to the said tabernacle, and to all other monuments of idolatry.[115]

From France, the Guises sent troops to help their kinswoman Mary stamp out the Protestant revolts. The Lords of the Congregation turned for help to Elizabeth, who had just succeeded her half-sister, Mary, as queen of England. Perhaps Knox regretted some of the words of his "trumpet blast" against female rulers, for he and Elizabeth found each other useful. Mary, Queen of Scots, had just become queen of France and was claiming rights to the throne of England. Neither Knox nor Elizabeth wished to see a strong Catholic on the throne of Scotland. Elizabeth sent ships to block the landing of French ships in Scottish harbors.

Mary of Lorraine died in 1560. Shortly thereafter, her daughter, representatives of the Congregation, and representatives of France and England signed the Treaty of Edinburgh. According to its terms, most of the French troops were to withdraw from Scotland; no Frenchman could hold high office; Mary was acknowledged queen of Scotland, but gave up her claim to the English throne; and Mary was forbidden to make war or peace without the consent of the now largely Protestant Scottish nobility. Although Scotland now had a Catholic queen, her power was severely limited.

In August 1560 Parliament accepted the Confession of Faith, a document drafted by Knox and his followers. Rejecting the authority of the pope and abolishing the Mass, the Confession became the official statement of belief and organization for the new Kirk (Church) of Scotland. It incorporated only two sacraments, baptism and communion, and embraced the Calvinist belief in predestination.

The Scottish form of Calvinism, called Presbyterianism, indicates by its name the central role of the presbyters, or elders, in running day-to-day affairs in the churches. Considered by Presbyterians too similar to Catholics in doctrine and organization, the Church of England, by contrast, is an episcopal church. That is, its high-ranking clergy are called bishops (*episcopus*, literally "overseer," is the Latin word for bishop). Anglican clergymen accompanied members of the Church of England to North America in the seventeenth century, forming, in the eighteenth century, the Protestant Episcopal Church in America; in 1973 the word *Protestant* was dropped from the name. North of the U.S.-Canada border, the denomination stemming from the Church of England is called the Anglican Church of Canada.

Puritans

One of the most influential antiepiscopal groups of the Reformation went by the name of Puritans. The Puritans were English Protestants who wanted to "purify" the English church and rid it of all elements that they considered "popish," that is, Roman Catholic. They believed in Calvinist doctrines such as predestination and election. In 1563 they first tried to pass a bill in Parliament eliminating "Romish" ceremonies. They objected to

Seeking freedom from religious persecution, English Puritans head for ships offshore that will take them to America.

Quaker Teaching

George Fox, founder of the Society of Friends (Quakers), summarizes Quaker teaching in this excerpt from his journals, dated about 1655, quoted in Christianity and Revolution: Radical Christian Testimonies, *edited by Lowell H. Zuck.*

"Now, when the Lord God and his son Jesus Christ, did send me forth into the world, to preach his everlasting gospel and kingdom, I was . . . commanded to turn people to that inward light, spirit and grace . . . even that divine Spirit which would lead them into all Truth. . . . I was to bring people off from all their own ways to Christ . . . and from their churches, which men had made and gathered, to the church in God. . . . And I was to bring people off. . . from men's inventions . . . with their schools and colleges for making ministers of Christ . . . and from all their images and crosses, and sprinkling [baptizing] of infants, with all their holy days (so called). . . . I was moved to declare against them all."

the wearing of vestments (special priestly robes), the making of the sign of the cross, the celebration of saints' days, and the use of music in church services. The proposal failed to pass, but the Puritans were undaunted.

The Puritans emphasized the direct authority of the Bible. Whereas the Lutherans and Anglicans believed that they could do anything that was not prohibited in the Bible, the Puritans believed that they could do *only* those things that Scripture specifically ordered or allowed. The Bible contains many contradictions, however, and Puritans sometimes disagreed over interpreting its directives.

The Puritans were willing to acknowledge Queen Elizabeth as head of the church in England as long as that meant keeping the pope out of their religious lives. However, as historians Will and Ariel Durant say, "in their hearts they rejected any control of religion by the state, and aspired to control of the state by their religion."[116]

Some Puritans pushed for a presbyterian form of church government in England, modeled on Knox's Kirk of Scotland. Others wanted to put all authority in the hands of individual congregations. The latter came to be called Separatists or Congregationalists. While most Puritans continued to worship in Church of England churches, Separatists defied the government by worshiping in their own churches. Elizabeth saw the Puritans' intensity and determination as a threat to the power of the throne and to her attempts to end religious strife in England. Eventually many Puritans fled to the more tolerant Holland, and later to America.

English religious leader George Fox founded the Society of Friends, or Quakers, in seventeenth-century England. The Quakers were persecuted for their rejection of organized churches and religious creeds.

Baptists, Quakers, and Other Offshoots of Puritanism

The Puritans' emphasis on interpreting the Bible literally led to deeper and wider divisions within the sect. It seemed that each time a group came up with an interpretation that contradicted an earlier one, a new sect appeared. During the seventeenth century, these mainly British offshoots of Puritanism multiplied rapidly. According to one writer of the time, in 1641 there were 29 separate sects in England. Five years later another writer listed 180 different sects. Two of the largest and most important of these groups were the Baptists and the Quakers.

Most Baptists held beliefs similar to the Separatist Puritans, but, like the Anabaptists, they did not believe in baptizing children. They found evidence in the Bible only for baptism of adults. Some believed in predestination; others did not. The Baptists, growing in numbers during the mid–seventeenth century, found a more receptive home in North America than they had in England.

The first Quakers were followers of an inspired preacher, George Fox. The Quakers eliminated almost all the formalities and customs of traditional religion and called themselves not a church but the Society of Friends. Indeed, they believed that individuals had direct access to God that did not require the help of the church or a minister or anything else.

Both Puritans and Anglicans felt threatened by the Quakers. All other existing forms of Christianity relied on the church and its ministers to help interpret the Bible and tell the people what behavior was expected of them. By the 1650s Quakers were leaving England in great numbers and immigrating to North America and the Caribbean islands.

The New Face of Europe and the World

No event marks the end of the Reformation in the way that the publication of Martin Luther's Ninety-five Theses marks the beginning. As we have seen, throughout the sixteenth century and into the seventeenth, new forms of Protestantism emerged and gradually became accepted. That trend continued through the eighteenth century and beyond. The Catholic Church regrouped at the Council of Trent, regained some of its lost territories, and swelled its numbers with new converts from Asia, India, and the Americas.

In 1600 Spain, France, Ireland, Italy, Austria, and most of eastern Europe remained Catholic. Scotland, parts of France and present-day Holland, Switzerland, pockets of northern Germany, and Hungary were Calvinist. Scandinavia, parts of the Netherlands, and most of Germany were Lutheran. England and northern Ireland were mostly Anglican. There were pockets of Anabaptism throughout Germany, the Low Countries, and eastern Europe.

Lasting Changes

The world after the Reformation has several features that distinguish it from the world before the Reformation. One is the availability of the Bible to ordinary people. Perhaps the printing press alone would have been enough to put Bibles into the hands of citizens everywhere, but the beliefs and zeal of the reformers also had a great deal to do with it. Translations of the Scriptures into every known language, the emphasis on individual interpretation, and the concept of the priesthood of all believers contributed to the proliferation of Bibles throughout Europe.

Some of the Bible translations are masterpieces of literature as well. Luther's German translation helped to shape the modern German language. Similarly, the English King James version (so named because it was the translation authorized by James I, who succeeded Elizabeth) greatly influenced the English language; its phrases have been familiar to the English-speaking world for almost four hundred years.

Another distinguishing feature of the post-Reformation world is the change in church architecture. The massive, elaborate cathedrals of the Late Middle Ages and the Renaissance gave way to smaller, less fancy church buildings. For Catholics, religious focus is on the celebration of the Mass, and so the altar at which the sacrament of communion is prepared has

(Left) Martin Luther will long be remembered as a brilliant theologian and inspirational leader. (Below) After the Reformation, the ornate cathedrals of the Late Middle Ages, such as St. Peter's (pictured), gave way to plainer, unadorned church buildings.

always been in the center of the church, in front of the people. The Protestant emphasis on Scripture and preaching led to churches whose focus was the pulpit, a narrow platform from which the minister read the Bible and preached to the people. The very plain, simple wooden and stone churches that are so common in New England and parts of the Midwest reflect directly the Puritan and Calvinist notion of simplicity and the imperative to avoid idolatry.

Before the Reformation, European Christians looked to the pope for authority. The Protestants turned instead to the authority of the Bible, and then splintered into many groups, each interpreting the Bible differently. But Protestants and Catholics alike found that local political authority grew stronger as the central authority of the church declined. Individual states or nations became more important as the formerly universal church became less powerful.

America

The very European experience of the Reformation had profound and lasting effects on the lands of North America, especially the region that would eventually become the United States. Many of the early American settlers left Europe specifically to find a place where they could practice their religion free from persecution. The Pilgrims who landed at Plymouth Rock in 1620 were Separatists who had emigrated once, from England to Holland, before resettling in the New World. They hoped to create a perfect colony devoted to God and a strict interpretation of the Scriptures. Their near neighbors were the less radical Puritans of the Massachusetts Bay Colony. Each group eventually found that to preserve religious freedom for itself, it had to extend the same right to others.

Roger Williams was a Puritan from Massachusetts Bay who wanted to eliminate all state control over the church. Historians describe this view: "Just as the pure church must be separate from a corrupt religious establishment, the church must also be totally separate from the state."[117] Faced with the choice between keeping silent about his beliefs and being deported from Massachusetts, Williams fled to what is now Rhode Island in early 1636 and set up his own colony, based on freedom of conscience and complete separation of church

Seeking religious freedom, settlers from Europe land on the American shore.

Religious Freedom in Pennsylvania

The colonists in the Americas were well aware of the dangers of religious intolerance. This excerpt from Pennsylvania's Charter of Privileges, dated October 28, 1701, is from Henry Steele Commager's Documents of American History.

"Because no people can be truly happy, though under the greatest enjoyment of Civil Liberties, if abridged of the Freedom of their Consciences, as to their Religious Profession and Worship . . . I [William Penn, governor of the province of Pennsylvania] do hereby grant and declare, that no Person or Persons, inhabiting in the province or Territories, who shall confess *One* almighty God, the Creator, Upholder and Ruler of the World; and profess him or themselves obliged to live quietly under the Civil Government, shall be in any Case molested or prejudiced, in his or their Person or Estate, because of his or their conscientious Persuasion or Practice, nor be compelled to frequent or maintain any religious Worship, Place or Ministry, contrary to his or their Mind, or to do or suffer any other Act or Thing, contrary to their religious Persuasion."

and state. He declared: "All men may walk as their consciences persuade them, every one in the name of his God."[118]

Rhode Island also provided a temporary home for Quakers, who had left Europe for the Caribbean island of Barbados and then attempted to settle in New England. Eventually the Quakers, under William Penn, set up a colony in what is now Pennsylvania.

Maryland gave a home to Roman Catholics, who were unwelcome in the stricter Protestant colonies. In 1649 Maryland became the first colony to grant religious freedom to all—at least to all Christians. The Lutherans congregated in Delaware and later in the upper Midwest. The Dutch Reformed Church was dominant in New York.

According to one account, in 1660 there were seventy-five Congregational (Separatist) churches in the American colonies, forty-one Anglican churches, thirteen Dutch Reformed, twelve Catholic, five Presbyterian, and four each Lutheran and Baptist. By the time of the Revolution, about 20 percent of the colonists were Congregationalist, 19 percent Presbyterian, 17 percent Baptist, 16 percent Episcopalian (the new American name for the Anglican Church), and 2 percent were Catholic.

A New Country

By the time of the drafting of the U.S. Constitution in the 1780s, it was clear that no single form of Christianity predominated in the colonies. As historian Mark Noll says, "Any effort to establish one particular faith would have drawn violent protests from adherents of other faiths." And yet, the colonists were overwhelmingly Protestant and overwhelmingly devoted to the concept that faith was an important part of life. The writers of the Constitution attempted to avoid the issue of religion altogether. Noll summarizes their dilemma: "If they were going to have a Constitution for all of the people, they somehow were going to have to get the government out of the religion business."[119]

Their solution appears in the Bill of Rights. The First Amendment to the Constitution begins: "Congress shall make no law respecting an establishment of religion, or prohibiting the free exercise thereof."

A More Tolerant World

The pre-Reformation Europe of one church became the post-Reformation Europe of many churches and of much greater separation of church and state. Religion developed a much more local or national character, which was true, as well, in the new colonies of America. Sometimes the differences led to intolerance, persecution, and war, problems that continue to plague society today. Nevertheless, a greater tolerance of differences began to grow. In the United States, people have freedom of worship, and there is no official state religion; partly because of the Reformation background of the early settlers, America became a place of refuge for freedom seekers around the world.

Notes

Chapter 1: Europe on the Eve of Reformation

1. Will Durant, *The Reformation*, vol. 6 of *The Story of Civilization*. New York: Simon & Schuster, 1957, p. 6.

2. Philip Hughes, *A Popular History of the Reformation*. Garden City, NY: Image Books, 1957, p. 13.

3. Harold J. Grimm, *The Reformation Era, 1500–1650*, 2nd ed. New York: Macmillan, 1973, p. 6.

4. Myron P. Gilmore, *The World of Humanism, 1453–1517*. New York: Harper & Row, 1952, p. 204.

5. Pico della Mirandola, *On the Dignity of Man*. Translated by Charles Glenn Wallis. New York: Bobbs Merrill, 1940, p. 22.

6. Quoted in Hughes, *A Popular History of the Reformation*, p. 48.

7. Durant, *The Reformation*, p. 8.

8. Quoted in Durant, *The Reformation*, p. 9.

9. Hughes, *A Popular History of the Reformation*, p. 101.

10. Quoted in Durant, *The Reformation*, p. 34.

11. Quoted in Durant, *The Reformation*, p. 165.

Chapter 2: "I Cannot Do Otherwise": Martin Luther

12. Quoted in Durant, *The Reformation*, p. 343.

13. Quoted in Hans J. Hillerbrand, *The World of the Reformation*. New York: Charles Scribner's Sons, 1973, p. 14.

14. Quoted in Hughes, *A Popular History of the Reformation*, p. 95.

15. Roland Bainton, *The Reformation of the Sixteenth Century*. Boston: Beacon Press, 1952, p. 24.

16. Rom. 1:17 Authorized (King James) Version.

17. Quoted in Hans J. Hillerbrand, ed., *The Reformation: A Narrative History Related by Contemporary Observers and Participants*. New York: Harper & Row, 1964, p. 44.

18. Quoted in Durant, *The Reformation*, p. 338.

19. Quoted in Durant, *The Reformation*, p. 339.

20. Quoted in Durant, *The Reformation*, p. 339.

21. Martin Luther, *Works*, gen. ed. Helmut T. Lehmann. Philadelphia: Muhlenberg Press, 1957–1962, vol. 41, p. 234.

22. Luther, *Works*, vol. 31, pp. 26–33.

23. Quoted in Durant, *The Reformation*, p. 348.

24. Quoted in Durant, *The Reformation*, p. 352.

25. Luther, *Works*, vol. 44, pp. 141–142.

26. Luther, *Works*, vol. 36, p. 18.

27. Luther, *Works*, vol. 31, p. 361.

28. Quoted in Hughes, *A Popular History of the Reformation*, p. 113.

29. Quoted in Grimm, *The Reformation Era*, p. 109.

30. Durant, *The Reformation*, p. 357.

31. Quoted in Grimm, *The Reformation Era*, p. 113.

32. Luther, *Works*, vol. 32, p. 110.

33. Luther, *Works*, vol. 32, p. 113.

34. Luther, *Works*, vol. 32, p. 113.

35. Quoted in Luther, *Works*, vol. 32, p. 115.

36. Luther, *Works*, vol. 48, p. 202.

Chapter 3: The King's "Great Matter": Reformation in England

37. Quoted in M. St. Clare Byrne, ed., *Letters of King Henry VIII*. New York: Funk & Wagnalls, 1936, p. 62.

38. Quoted in J. J. Scarisbrick, *Henry VIII*. Berkeley: University of California Press, 1968, p. 181.

39. Quoted in Durant, *The Reformation*, p. 528.

40. Quoted in Byrne, *Letters of King Henry VIII*, p. 63.

41. *The Famous History of the Life of King Henry VIII*, act 2, scene 2, The Cambridge Edition Text. Garden City, NY: Garden City Books, 1936.

42. Quoted in Durant, *The Reformation*, p. 551.

43. Quoted in Durant, *The Reformation*, p. 532.

44. Quoted in W. E. Campbell, ed., *The Last Letters*

of Blessed Thomas More. St. Louis, MO: Herder, 1924, p. 28.

45. Quoted in Scarisbrick, *Henry VIII,* p. 290.

46. Quoted in Hughes, *A Popular History of the Reformation,* p. 169.

47. Quoted in Henry Bettenson, ed., *Documents of the Christian Church.* London: Oxford University Press, 1963, p. 218.

48. Quoted in Bettenson, *Documents of the Christian Church,* p. 218.

49. Hughes, *A Popular History of the Reformation,* p. 171.

50. Quoted in Bettenson, *Documents of the Christian Church,* p. 227.

Chapter 4: Reformers Become Protestants

51. Quoted in Durant, *The Reformation,* p. 386.

52. Quoted in Owen Chadwick, *The Reformation.* New York: Penguin Books, 1968, p. 62.

53. Chadwick, *The Reformation,* p. 62.

54. Quoted in Bettenson, *Documents of the Christian Church,* p. 211.

55. Psalms 19:12 AV.

56. Grimm, *The Reformation Era,* p. 148.

57. Quoted in Durant, *The Reformation,* p. 408.

58. Grimm, *The Reformation,* p. 153.

59. Quoted in Durant, *The Reformation,* p. 463.

60. Quoted in Hillerbrand, *The World of the Reformation,* p. 75.

61. Quoted in Durant, *The Reformation,* p. 465.

Chapter 5: Changing Europe: Society During the Reformation

62. Quoted in Durant, *The Reformation,* p. 866.

63. Raymond Sokolov, *Why We Eat What We Eat: How the Encounter Between the New World and the Old Changed the Way Everyone on the Planet Eats.* New York: Summit Books, 1991, p. 13.

64. Quoted in Durant, *The Reformation,* p. 159.

65. Quoted in Durant, *The Reformation,* p. 159.

66. Quoted in Lewis W. Spitz, *The Protestant Reformation, 1517–1559.* New York: Harper & Row, 1985, p. 89.

67. Quoted in Spitz, *The Protestant Reformation,* p. 90.

68. Spitz, *The Protestant Reformation,* p. 91.

69. Quoted in Durant, *The Reformation,* p. 358.

70. Spitz, *The Protestant Reformation,* p. 360.

71. Luther, *Works,* vol. 44, pp. 142–143.

72. Quoted in Durant, *The Reformation,* p. 778.

73. Quoted in Durant, *The Reformation,* p. 786.

74. Quoted in Luther, *Works,* vol. 54, p. 359.

75. Quoted in Natalie Z. Davis, *Society and Culture in Early Modern France: Eight Essays.* Stanford, CA: Stanford University Press, 1975, p. 92.

76. Luther, *Works,* vol. 54, p. 8.

77. Luther, *Works,* vol. 41, p. 154.

78. Davis, *Society and Culture in Early Modern France,* p. 92.

Chapter 6: Religious Wars and Persecution

79. Quoted in Hillerbrand, *The Reformation: A Narrative History,* p. 125.

80. Luther, *Works,* vol. 49, p. 179.

81. Quoted in Spitz, *The Protestant Reformation,* p. 161.

82. Durant, *The Reformation,* p. 580.

83. Quoted in Spitz, *The Protestant Reformation,* p. 278.

84. Bainton, *The Reformation of the Sixteenth Century,* p. 165.

85. Bainton, *The Reformation of the Sixteenth Century,* p. 169.

86. Quoted in Bainton, *The Reformation of the Sixteenth Century,* pp. 169–170.

87. Quoted in Chadwick, *The Reformation,* p. 164.

88. Quoted in Bettenson, *Documents of the Christian Church,* p. 216.

89. Quoted in Bainton, *The Reformation of the Sixteenth Century,* p. 211.

90. Quoted in Bainton, *The Reformation of the Sixteenth Century,* p. 214.

91. Bainton, *The Reformation of the Sixteenth Century,* p. 218.

92. Quoted in Bainton, *The Reformation of the Sixteenth Century,* p. 224.

93. Quoted in Bainton, *The Reformation of the Sixteenth Century*, p. 226.

Chapter 7: The Catholic Response: Counter-Reformation

94. Hughes, *A Popular History of the Reformation*, p. 83.

95. Hughes, *A Popular History of the Reformation*, p. 83.

96. Spitz, *The Protestant Reformation*, p. 304.

97. Quoted in Anthony E. Gilles, *The People of Anguish: The Story Behind the Reformation*. Cincinnati: St. Anthony Messenger Press, 1987, p. 168.

98. Gilles, *The People of Anguish*, p. 168.

99. Durant, *The Reformation*, p. 9.

100. Quoted in Gilles, *The People of Anguish*, p. 102.

101. Quoted in Durant, *The Reformation*, p. 920.

102. Quoted in Durant, *The Reformation*, p. 922.

103. Quoted in Durant, *The Reformation*, p. 925.

104. Quoted in Durant, *The Reformation*, p. 925.

105. Durant, *The Reformation*, p. 926.

106. Jas. 2:26. AV.

107. Durant, *The Reformation*, p. 929.

108. Gilles, *The People of Anguish*, p. 116.

Chapter 8: The Reformation Spreads

109. Quoted in Bettenson, *Documents of the Christian Church*, p. 215.

110. Chadwick, *The Reformation*, p. 169.

111. Quoted in Spitz, *The Protestant Reformation*, p. 230.

112. Quoted in Spitz, *The Protestant Reformation*, p. 280.

113. Quoted in Marvin A. Breslow, ed., *The Political Writings of John Knox*. Washington, DC: Folger Books, 1985, p. 42.

114. Quoted in Durant, *The Reformation*, p. 615.

115. Quoted in Durant, *The Reformation*, p. 616.

116. Will and Ariel Durant, *The Age of Reason Begins*, vol. 7 of *The Story of Civilization*. New York: Simon & Schuster, 1961, p. 23.

Epilogue: The New Face of Europe and the World

117. Charles H. Lippy, Robert Choquette, and Stafford Poole, *Christianity Comes to the Americas*. New York: Paragon House, 1992, p. 276.

118. Quoted in Lippy, Choquette, and Poole, *Christianity Comes to the Americas*, p. 277.

119. Mark A. Noll, *A History of Christianity in the United States and Canada*. Grand Rapids, MI: Eerdmans, 1992, p. 145.

Glossary

apostolic: having to do with the apostles, the first followers of Jesus of Nazareth.

bishop: a high-ranking church official; usually in charge of a particular area called a diocese.

cardinal: one of the small and elite group of bishops responsible for electing the pope.

clergy: people ordained for religious service; priests, ministers, etc.

clerical: relating to the clergy.

communion: Eucharist; the sacrament of receiving consecrated bread and wine of which Jesus said, "This is my body; this is my blood." There are many different interpretations about the relationship of the bread and wine to the actual body and blood of Jesus.

confession: also called the sacrament of reconciliation, or penance; the act by which a person tells or confesses his or her sins to a priest, who is then authorized to give absolution (forgiveness).

diet: a formal general assembly of the princes and lords of the Holy Roman Empire.

electors: the princes, lords, and dukes who were in charge of the provinces of the Holy Roman Empire; they were responsible for electing the Holy Roman Emperor.

Eucharist: the sacrament of communion, from the Greek word for thanksgiving.

excommunication: a formal punishment that excludes a person from participation in the sacraments and from the life of the church.

heresy: any statement or act that contradicts the teachings of the church.

heretic: a person who commits heresy.

Holy Roman Empire: a loosely federated political entity of central Europe. In the sixteenth century, it was composed of the German-speaking states, Spain, and parts of northern Italy.

humanism: a cultural and intellectual movement of the Renaissance that emphasized human beings and their needs and values, based on a study of literature, art, and the civilizations of ancient Greece and Rome.

humanist: a Renaissance scholar devoted to humanism.

indulgence: document granting release from God's punishment due for human sins after the holder of the indulgence has been forgiven by a priest or bishop.

Mass: the common name for the Catholic church service, which always includes celebration of the sacrament of communion.

monk: a man who is a member of a brotherhood, living in or reporting to a monastery and following a particular discipline; a monk may or may not be a priest (that is, authorized to administer the sacraments), depending on his education and training.

papacy: the office of the pope.

papal: having to do with the pope.

Papal States: a group of territories in central Italy ruled by the popes from 754 until 1870.

penance: an act performed voluntarily to

show sorrow for a sin or other act of wrongdoing; also, the sacrament of confession.

pope: today, head of the Roman Catholic Church; in pre-Reformation days, the pope was the head of European Christendom.

prelate: a high-ranking member of the clergy, usually a bishop.

sacrament: a visible form of invisible grace, instituted by Jesus. The Catholic Church recognizes seven of these, each with its rites and ceremonies: baptism, confirmation, Eucharist (communion), reconciliation (confession), holy orders, marriage, and the anointing of the sick. Most Protestant churches recognize only two: baptism and communion.

salvation: the condition of being saved, being freed from sin and its effects, and being reconciled with God; especially, having eternal life in heaven after death.

For Further Reading

Robert Bolt, *A Man for All Seasons: A Play in Two Acts*. New York: Vintage Books, 1960. A wonderful play about the conflict between Henry VIII and Thomas More over the king's desire to divorce his wife and leave the church. The play was made into an Academy Award–winning film in 1964 starring Paul Scofield and Robert Shaw. It is available on videocassette.

Catherine Bush, *Elizabeth I*. New York: Chelsea House, 1985. The firm establishment of the Anglican Church occurred during Elizabeth's reign, as did the creation of Puritanism. This biography deals with those issues as part of Elizabeth's life and reign. Numerous illustrations.

Trevor Cairns, *The Birth of Modern Europe*. Minneapolis: Lerner Publications, 1975. Places the Reformation in the context of other social and political changes in Europe between 1500 and 1715.

Leonard W. Cowie, *The Reformation*. New York: John Day, 1967. A straightforward account of the Reformation period. Contains black-and-white illustrations.

Frank Dwyer, *Henry VIII*. New York: Chelsea House, 1988. This biography details Henry's marriage problems and his break with the Roman Catholic Church. Many illustrations.

Winifred Roll, *Mary I: The History of an Unhappy Tudor Queen*. Englewood Cliffs, NJ: Prentice-Hall, 1980. Drawing largely on papers and documents from the sixteenth century, this book presents an unbiased look at the life and the brief and troubled reign of Mary I.

Edith Simon and the Time-Life Books editors, *The Reformation*, Great Ages of Man Series. Alexandria, VA: Time-Life Books, 1966. An excellent brief overview of the Reformation period. Many illustrations and sidebars on such aspects as printing, art, and banking.

Sally Stepanek, *John Calvin*. New York: Chelsea House, 1987. A straightforward and entertaining biography of one of the great Reformation theologians and leaders.

Sally Stepanek, *Martin Luther*. New York: Chelsea House, 1986. A thorough, fair, and interesting accounting of the life of this important Reformation leader.

Sally Stepanek, *Mary, Queen of Scots*. New York: Chelsea House, 1987. Much of Mary's reign centered around the conflict between Catholicism and Protestantism in Scotland and England. This biography presents that conflict in the context of the queen's life.

Time-Life Books editors, *The European Emergence: TimeFrame AD 1500–1800*. Alexandria, VA: Time-Life Books, 1989. Discusses the Reformation and its effect in Europe. Also provides an excellent discussion of the rest of the world in the sixteenth and seventeenth centuries, particularly Russia, the Ottoman Empire, and India and China. Many excellent color pictures and maps.

Jane Yolen, *Friend: The Story of George Fox and the Quakers*. New York: Seabury Press, 1972. This biography by award-winning author Jane Yolen tells the story of Quaker George Fox, one of the most fascinating characters of the later Reformation period.

Works Consulted

Roland Bainton, *The Reformation of the Sixteenth Century*. Boston: Beacon Press, 1952. A classic work of the Reformation period by a Protestant historian.

Henry Bettenson, ed., *Documents of the Christian Church*. London: Oxford University Press, 1963. An informative collection of original documents from the early church to the present.

Owen Chadwick, *The Reformation*. New York: Penguin Books, 1968. A complete and evenhanded approach to the entire Reformation period.

Natalie Z. Davis, *Society and Culture in Early Modern France: Eight Essays*. Stanford, CA: Stanford University Press, 1975. Davis concentrates on the history of everyday life and common people, especially women, in this collection of essays. Of particular interest is the essay "City Women and Religious Change."

Will Durant, *The Reformation*. Vol. 6 of *The Story of Civilization*. New York: Simon & Schuster, 1957. A scholarly and entertaining survey of the Reformation period up to the mid-1500s. Durant presents a balanced account of both Catholic and Protestant sides of events.

Will and Ariel Durant, *The Age of Reason Begins*. Vol. 7 of *The Story of Civilization*. New York: Simon & Schuster, 1961. Although this volume of the Durants' history of civilization concentrates on the Enlightenment period, it also includes events of the Reformation from the mid-1500s on.

Anthony J. Gilles, *The People of Anguish: The Story Behind the Reformation*. Cincinnati: St. Anthony Messenger Press, 1987. A highly readable volume in this Catholic historian's People of God Series about the history of the church.

Myron P. Gilmore, *The World of Humanism, 1453–1517*. New York: Harper & Row, 1952. A scholarly account of the world at the outset of the Reformation period.

Harold J. Grimm, *The Reformation Era, 1500–1650*. 2nd ed. New York: Macmillan, 1973. One of the most thorough and evenhanded approaches to the Reformation period. Very readable and entertaining as well as scholarly.

Hans J. Hillerbrand, *The World of the Reformation*. New York: Charles Scribner's Sons, 1973. Hillerbrand concentrates on the social aspects of the Reformation—how it affected people's lives.

Hans J. Hillerbrand, ed. *The Reformation: A Narrative History Related by Contemporary Observers and Participants*. New York: Harper & Row, 1964. This is a delightful compilation of firsthand accounts of events surrounding the Reformation. Hillerbrand introduces each account and places each in historical perspective.

Philip Hughes, *A Popular History of the Reformation*. Garden City, NY: Image Books, 1957. Hughes, a well-known and highly respected Jesuit historian, presents the Reformation from the Catholic perspective.

Charles H. Lippy, Robert Choquette, and Stafford Poole, *Christianity Comes to the Americas*. New York: Paragon House, 1992. Shows both Catholic and Protestant influences in the Americas from 1492 to 1776.

Martin Luther, *Works*. General editor Helmut T. Lehmann. 55 vols. Philadelphia: Muhlenberg Press, 1957–1962. This massive work of many editors and translators gives an idea of the sheer quantity of work that Martin Luther produced in his lifetime. Items are introduced and footnoted to place them in the context of Luther's life and work.

Mark A. Noll, *A History of Christianity in the United States and Canada*. Grand Rapids, MI: Eerdmans, 1992. This book shows the European background of the various religious groups that settled in North America.

J. J. Scarisbrick, *Henry VIII*. Berkeley: University of California Press, 1968. An entertaining and thorough biography.

Raymond Sokolov, *Why We Eat What We Eat: How the Encounter Between the New World and the Old Changed the Way Everyone on the Planet Eats*. New York: Summit Books, 1991. A fascinating and entertaining history of food that focuses on the changes that came about in the sixteenth century as a result of the voyages of exploration.

Lewis W. Spitz, *The Protestant Reformation, 1517–1559*. New York: Harper & Row, 1985. This noted Protestant historian presents a scholarly, well-written account of the Reformation's most dynamic years.

Additional Works Consulted

Marvin A. Breslow, ed., *The Political Writings of John Knox*. Washington: Folger Books, 1985.

M. St. Clare Byrne, ed., *Letters of King Henry VIII*. New York: Funk & Wagnalls, 1936.

W. E. Campbell, ed., *The Last Letters of Blessed Thomas More*. St. Louis, MO: Herder, 1924.

Henry Steele Commager, ed., *Documents of American History*. New York: Appleton-Century-Crofts, 1973.

Charles Dollen, ed., *Prayer Book of the Saints*. Huntington, IN: Our Sunday Visitor, 1984.

Desiderius Erasmus, *Julius Exclusus*. Translated by Paul Pascal. Bloomington, IN: Indiana University Press, 1968.

Henry Emerson Fosdick, ed., *Great Voices of the Reformation: An Anthology*. New York: Modern Library, 1952.

John Foxe, *Foxe's Book of English Martyrs*. Edited by Hilda Noel Schroetter. Waco, TX: Word Books, 1981.

John Gerard, *The Autobiography of a Hunted Priest*. Translated from the Latin by Philip Caraman. New York: Image Books, 1955.

Methodist Hymnal. Baltimore, MD: Methodist Publishing House, 1939.

Pico della Mirandola, *On the Dignity of Man*. Translated by Charles Glenn Wallis. New York: Bobbs Merrill, 1940.

Thomas More, *Utopia*. Translated and edited by H. V. S. Ogden. New York: Appleton-Century-Crofts, 1949.

Lowell H. Zuck, ed., *Christianity and Revolution: Radical Christian Testimonies, 1520–1650*. Philadelphia: Temple University Press, 1975.

Index

Picture Credits

Cover photo by AKG, Berlin

The Bettmann Archive, 11, 20, 26, 51, 58, 60, 75, 77, 101

Culver Pictures, 44, 49, 76, 81, 90, 91 (right), 99 (top)

Library of Congress, 17, 23, 24, 37 (bottom), 40, 54, 63 (both), 65, 70, 71, 92, 108 (top), 109

North Wind Picture Archives, 13, 14, 18, 22, 25, 33, 68 (right), 88, 89, 91 (left), 106, 108 (bottom)

Stock Montage, 29, 34, 41, 43, 62, 82, 83, 99 (bottom), 103

About the Author

Sarah Flowers is a writer and a librarian. She holds a B.A. degree from Kansas State University, an M.A. degree from the University of California (Berkeley), and an M.L.S. from San Jose State University. She has always been interested in history and in writing for young people, and has had articles published in a number of magazines including *Cricket* and *Parenting*. She is currently the Young Adult Services Librarian at Los Gatos (CA) Public Library. This is her first book. She lives in Morgan Hill, California, with her husband and their three sons.